Lou Gehrig

One of Baseball's Greatest

Illustrated by Jerry Robinson

Lou Gehrig

One of Baseball's Greatest

by Guernsey Van Riper
Illustrated by Paul Laune

THE BOBBS-MERRILL COMPANY, INC.
INDIANAPOLIS/NEW YORK

COPYRIGHT © 1949, 1959 BY THE BOBBS-MERRILL CO., INC.
ALL RIGHTS RESERVED

No part of this publication may be reproduced, stored in a retrieval system or transmitted in any form or by any means, mechanical, electronic, photocopying, recording or otherwise without the prior written permission of the publisher. For information, address The Bobbs-Merrill Co., Inc., 630 Third Avenue, New York, NY 10017

PUBLISHED BY THE BOBBS-MERRILL CO., INC.
INDIANAPOLIS/NEW YORK
MANUFACTURED IN THE UNITED STATES OF AMERICA

Library of Congress Cataloging in Publication Data

Van Riper, Guernsey, 1909—
  Lou Gehrig, one of baseball's greatest.

(Childhood of famous Americans)
New ed. of: Lou Gehrig, boy of the sandlots. 1959.
Summary: A biography focusing on the childhood of one of the greatest professional baseball players who is remembered for playing 2,130 consecutive games in 14 seasons with the New York Yankees.
1. Gehrig, Lou, 1903–1941—Juvenile literature.
2. Baseball players—United States—Biography—Juvenile literature.
3. New York Yankees (Baseball team)—Juvenile literature.

[1. Gehrig, Lou, 1903–1941. 2. Baseball players]   I. Laune, Paul, ill.   II. Title.   III. Series.
GV865.G4V36   1982   796.357′092′4 [B]   82-1296
ISBN 0-672-52734-0   [92]   AACR2

*To every youngster everywhere
who loves the game of baseball*

Illustrations

Full pages

	PAGE
Louie dashed up the stairs.	23
There was Louie, safe and sound.	78
"Three for a nickel!"	101
"What's going on here?"	136
Lou studied on the streetcar.	145
Lou made the winning home run.	173

Numerous smaller illustrations

Contents

	PAGE		PAGE
"Merry Christmas!"	11	Lou Goes to High School	103
Let's Play Ball	20	Trouble in School	130
Louie Learns a Lesson	42	Lou Earns Five Dollars	139
The Boys Get into Mischief	59	City Champions	149
		The Big Game	160
Louie Makes the Team	81	The Yankee Slugger	175
Fun for Mom and Louie	88	"The Greatest Example"	185

Books by Guernsey Van Riper, Jr.

BABE RUTH: BASEBALL BOY
JIM THORPE: INDIAN ATHLETE
KNUTE ROCKNE: YOUNG ATHLETE
LOU GEHRIG: BOY OF THE SANDLOTS
RICHARD BYRD: BOY OF THE SOUTH POLE
WILL ROGERS: YOUNG COWBOY

Lou Gehrig

One of Baseball's Greatest

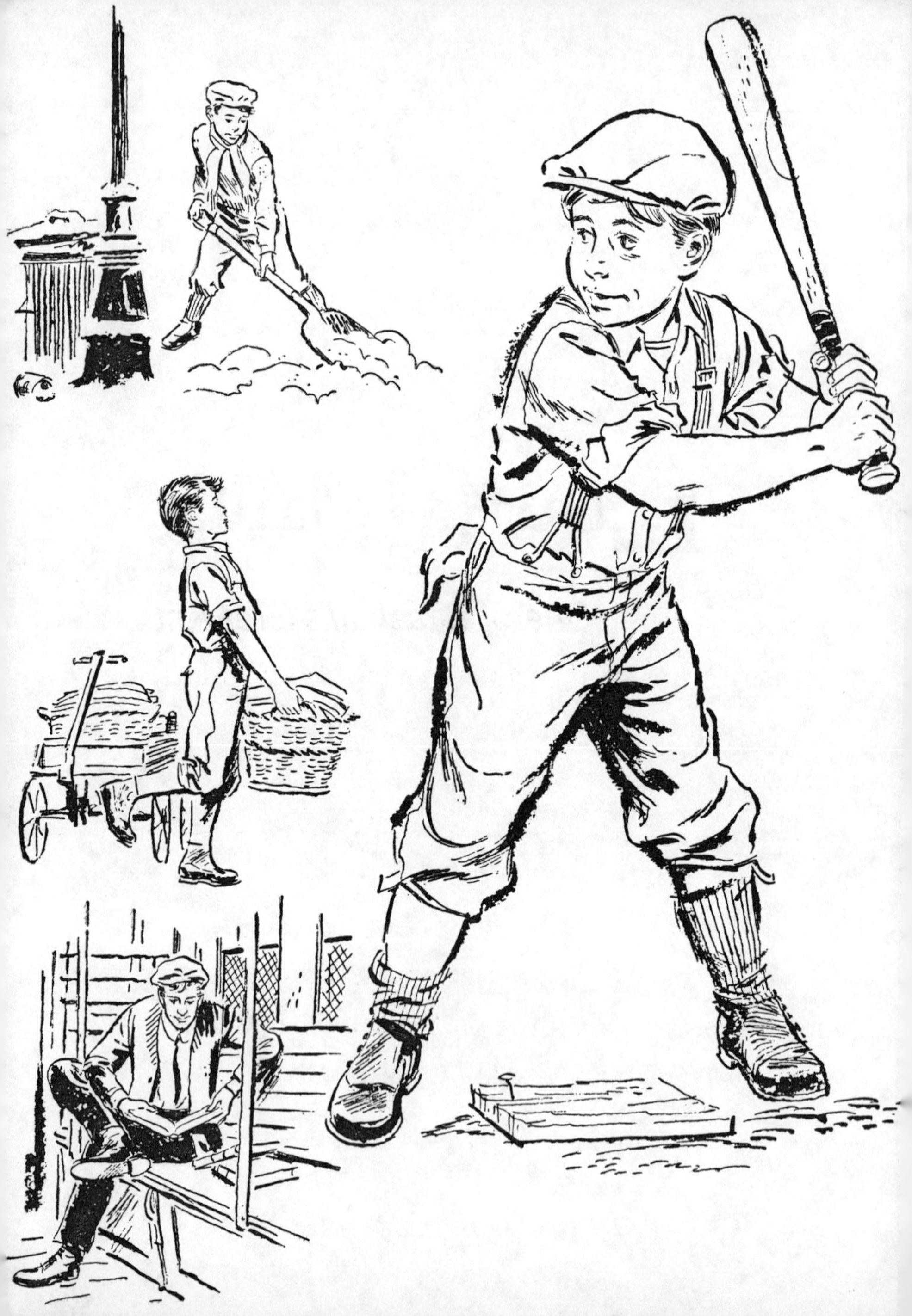

"Merry Christmas!"

"S-SH!" SAID Mom Gehrig. Two fat walnuts clattered on the bare floor.

"S-sh!" said Pop Gehrig.

He picked them up carefully and put them in a stocking hanging from the edge of the table. The stocking was shabby, and darned in many places, but now it looked interesting. It bulged here and it bulged there. It was full of oranges and nuts and Christmas cookies.

"Don't wake Louie!" whispered Mom Gehrig.

She tied a red paper bell on the branch of a small pine tree standing on the table. It was a very tiny pine tree. In fact, it was really the tip-top of a huge tree that had to be cut off before it would go indoors. But Mom Gehrig was glad to have the small piece. She felt pleased that she had been walking along Fifth Avenue when the tiny tree was about to be thrown out. Maybe it wouldn't have looked so nice in one of the big houses on the Avenue, but in the little Gehrig apartment it was just right.

Just then there was a noisy clatter outside. A streetcar rushed past.

"I guess if the streetcars don't wake him, these walnuts won't," said Pop. "New York is not a very quiet place to live."

In the next room Louie stirred in his sleep. He was used to streetcars, but he *had* heard the walnuts fall. Still, he was sleeping so soundly it took him a long time to wake up. Finally he opened his eyes.

"It's Christmas Eve!" he thought with sudden excitement.

Louie pushed back the covers. He swung his feet over the edge of his cot. He crept over to the door as quietly as he could. Carefully he avoided the low sink piled with clean dishes. He slept in the kitchen. His parents slept in the other room. Very softly he opened the door a little. He peeped through the crack.

He was surprised to see Mom and Pop. They weren't in bed! Then he saw the little tree and the stocking. "Santa Claus has already been here!" he thought. The next minute he forgot about Santa Claus. He forgot about everything—everything except the beautiful object lying on the table.

It wasn't... it couldn't be... but there it was! A real baseball glove! A catcher's mitt! For him!

Louie was only five years old, going on six, that Christmas of 1908. He had wished for a baseball glove for a long, long time. He really never expected to have one. They cost so much. Mom and Pop worked hard, but they never had extra money for things like toys or baseball gloves. They had to spend all their money just for things that were needed.

Louie's eyes were glued to the crack. He studied every detail of that catcher's mitt. He almost burst into the room. He wanted to hold the mitt in his hands and try it on. He whacked it with his fist and pretended he was really catching at home plate, like the older boys he had watched.

Now he'd show the gang! Now they wouldn't keep him out of their games because he was too young. Oh, he'd let them all use the mitt, of course. They'd like it as much as he would. But now they would let him play, too!

Just as he was about to push through the door, Louie remembered. "Mom told me to stay in bed till morning. She wouldn't like it if I went in there now."

Very unwillingly he crawled back into bed. He wondered if Mom and Pop had seen Santa Claus bring the tree and fill the stocking. He went back to sleep dreaming of the wonderful catcher's mitt and everything he would do with it. Before he knew it, morning had come.

At six o'clock Louie slipped out of bed. He

was in such a hurry he could hardly get his clothes on.

Then Mom came in. "Merry Christmas, Louie!" She beamed.

"Merry Christmas, Mom!" said Louie.

"Come in and see what Santa Claus brought!"

Santa Claus! Louie wanted to ask if Mom and Pop had seen him. But then he shouldn't have been peeking. Should he ask? Yes, he could tell Mom what he had seen. He could always tell her the truth.

"Mom," he said timidly, "did you see Santa Claus? Did you see him come? I ... I woke up and peeked in and saw the tree and stocking and ... everything."

Mom Gehrig was thunderstruck. She thought, "Those walnuts! Oh, but Pop was clumsy!" Then she said, "No, Louie, we weren't quick enough. But we heard him! So we got up to see what he brought. Come in now and see for yourself!"

Louie shot into the next room. In a moment he had the catcher's mitt in his hands. It was a beauty! He rubbed the cool leather. Then he put it on. It was wonderful! He thumped it and thumped it. He held it up and pretended to be catching a high fly.

Then he pretended to throw a ball to second, and he thought, "This is funny. Something is wrong with this mitt."

He always threw with his left hand, but the catcher's mitt fitted his left hand instead of his right. Since he was left-handed, he always caught with his right hand.

He tried putting the mitt on his right hand. It didn't fit very well, for the big padded thumb was on the wrong side. Still, it was a beauty, and it was *his!* Somehow he'd make it work. Besides, all the other kids were right-handed. It would fit them fine.

He started to tell Mom and Pop, but then

he thought, "Santa Claus might hear me, and he wouldn't like it."

Then, too, Mom and Pop just didn't understand baseball. Louie looked over to where they were watching him. They were smiling and nodding their heads.

"It must be a good one," said Mom.

"This baseball is very important in America," said Pop, "and Louie is a real little American, he likes it so much."

"I was born right here in New York, wasn't I, Mom?" Louie chimed in.

"Yes, Louie, and you're a lucky boy," said his mother. "Your Pop and I had to come all the way across the ocean to the United States. But we came to find good work where everybody has a chance, not to play baseball!"

"Now, Christina!" said Pop. He and Louie laughed at the idea of Mom playing baseball.

"Well, if Louie likes it, it will keep him busy

when we have to be away from home working," agreed Mom good-naturedly.

Louie placed a sofa pillow on the floor. He stood behind it in a crouch. He held out his hands just the way the other boys did. "Shoot one over the plate!" he shouted. He thumped the new mitt.

Let's Play Ball

Louie Gehrig marched straight up Amsterdam Avenue. He was clutching three quarters tightly in his pocket. He was pulling a rickety little wagon. He stopped carefully at the corner of 169th Street to let a horse-drawn cart rumble past. Then he crossed quickly and trotted along the last block toward home.

It was a bright, windy day in March. There was a touch of spring in the air. It was the first pleasant day after a cold, snowy winter. Louie heard shouts and trotted faster. Yes! There, in the vacant lot on the corner, was the neighborhood gang. They were tossing a baseball around. Ever since Christmas Louie had been waiting for this.

As he came closer, he heard Willie yell, "Come on, let's start a game! First bat!"

There were shouts of "Catcher!" "Pitcher!" "First base!" "Second base!"

Tony called out, "Hey, we need some more. We haven't got any outfielders!"

Then Goose spied Louie. "Here comes Fat Gehrig," he shouted. "That's one more."

"Aw, we don't want him. He's too young to play," said Harold.

"Sure, Louie doesn't even go to school yet," Tony agreed. "We want somebody bigger."

By this time Louie had reached the door of the apartment building where he lived. He was glad to hear Willie say, "Oh, let him play. He's bigger than you are, Tony. Hey, come on out, Louie."

Louie left the wagon in the hall. He rushed

21

to a door and knocked. A pleasant-looking woman answered. He said, "I left your wagon by the door, Mrs. Riley. Thank you very much for letting me use it again."

"You're welcome to it any time, Louie," Mrs. Riley said. "My children have grown so big they don't use it——Goodness!"

Louie hadn't waited to hear what she was saying. He had rushed to the stairs and was already half way up the first flight.

Mrs. Riley shook her head. "I never saw him in such a hurry before," she said as she went back into her apartment.

Louie dashed up to the fourth floor, two steps at a time. The Gehrigs' two small rooms were at the far end of the hall. He burst into the apartment, where his mother was busy ironing.

"Mom! Oh, Mom!" he called.

Mom looked up from the ironing board. "Well, Louie, you weren't gone very long," she said.

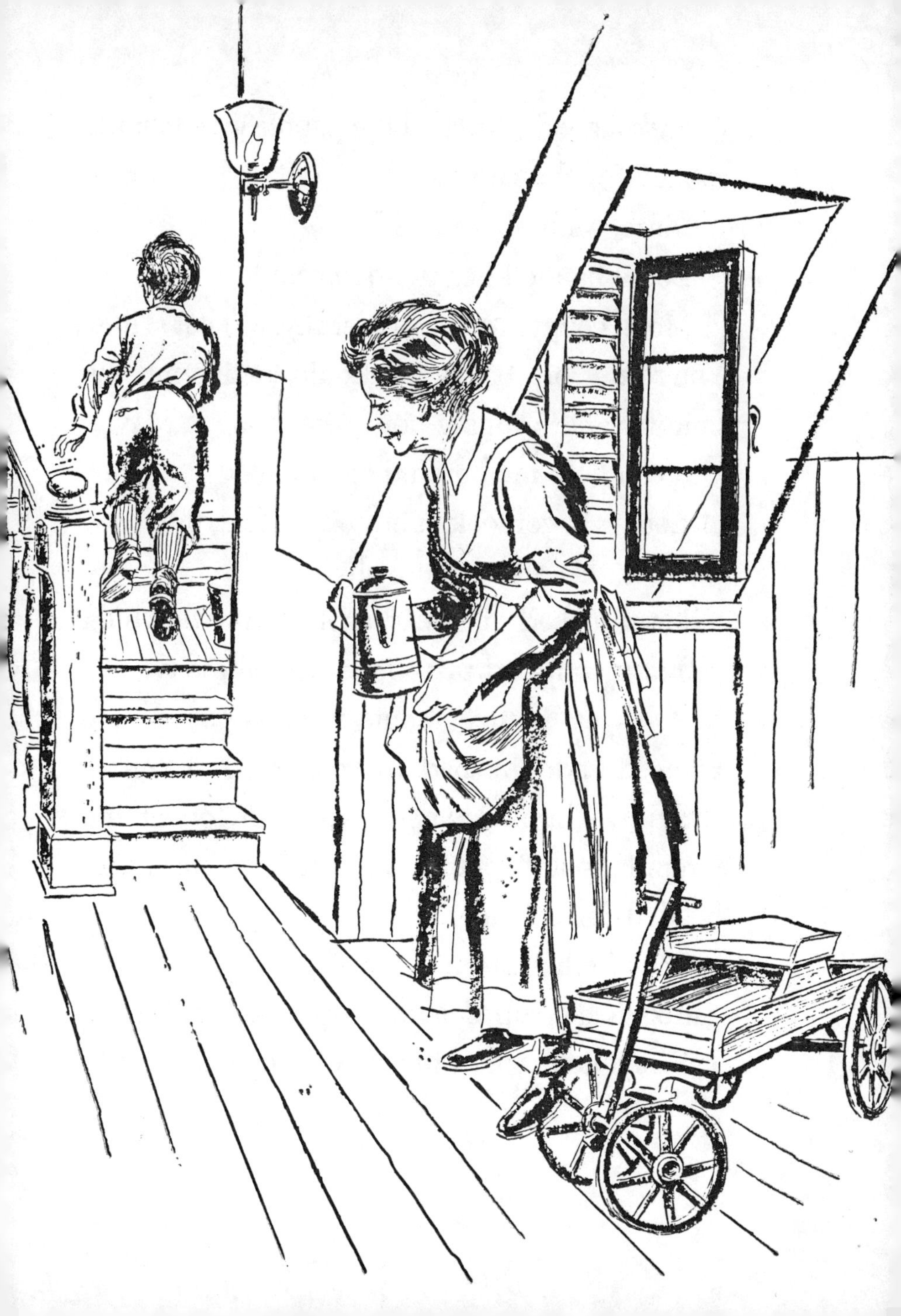

"That's a good boy. Did the people give you the money for the laundry?"

"Sure, Mom, here it is."

Louie handed her the quarters.

Mom counted them carefully. "That's fine. You're my big boy now, Louie, delivering the laundry and bringing home the money. Maybe you can help me here a little more."

Louie's eager look vanished, but he didn't say a word. He stood there shyly.

Mom looked at him sharply. "Maybe you'd rather go out and play on such a fine day?"

"Oh, yes, Mom!" Louie was overjoyed. He reached under his bed and pulled out a bundle carefully wrapped in newspaper. He tore off the wrappings and put on his catcher's mitt. He headed for the door.

"You be back in time for supper," his mother called as he rushed out.

When he reached the street, Louie slowed to

a walk. As he came to the lot, Tony set up a shout. "Look what Fat's got! A catcher's mitt! A real catcher's mitt!"

In an instant the game stopped. A group of curious boys surrounded Louie.

"Where'd you get it?"

"How come we haven't seen it before?"

"You let us use the mitt, and you can watch."

Louie said firmly, "Sure, you can all use it. But I want to play, too."

Harold shouted, "What have you got it on your right hand for? You don't even know how to play!"

Goose said, "Aw, he's just a fat kid. Come on, take his glove and let's play."

Louie blushed bright red. He would have liked to say that he wasn't fat, but he just stood his ground and held onto his mitt. He grinned up at Willie, though he felt uncomfortable.

"Might as well let him play," said Willie good-naturedly. "Here, let me catch with your glove. You go on out to right field."

Delightedly Louie handed over his glove and trotted out to right field. He even dared to shout, "Come on, batter up!"

He had never been so happy. Here he was, really playing baseball. Every time a batter swung at the ball, Louie got ready to catch it. But none came his way.

Finally he moved up to pitcher. Willie was batting. Louie took the ball and threw it with all his might toward the plate. Willie took a hard swing, but missed.

"Would you look at that!" shouted Harold. "Louie's a lefty!"

"He sure throws like a cow," Goose chimed in.

Louie threw another. Willie hit a little pop fly to Tony, who caught it easily. Louie ran in joyfully and picked up the catcher's mitt. He was smiling broadly. "Shoot one over the plate," he shouted to Harold, who was now pitching.

Louie thumped his mitt and tried to crouch down like a real catcher. The mitt was awkward on his right hand, but he didn't mind. Harold threw the ball hard and straight, a good strike.

27

As the batter swung, Louie flinched back a little. When the batter missed, Louie wasn't ready. The ball hit him in the stomach. He sat down with a thud.

A howl of laughter went up over the field. "Would you look at that!" shouted Harold. "He doesn't need a mitt. He's fat enough to use his stomach!" Harold joined in the laughing.

Louie got to his feet and just smiled. He'd do better next time. When Harold threw a wide ball, Louie quickly reached out his mitt. *Plunk!* He had it. It felt good. He tossed it back to Harold. He even managed to say, "Throw him a strike now, Harold."

Harold threw it right over. The batter swung hard, but just nicked it. The ball trickled back to the pitcher. Harold picked it up easily and threw it to the first baseman. "You're out!" he shouted. "Come on, Louie, move up! You're at bat now." He dropped his glove by the pitcher's mound and ran for home plate. All the other boys moved forward a place, too.

Louie picked up the bat uneasily. At last it was his turn. Hesitantly he took one practice swing, then another.

"Here's an easy out," shouted Goose. "Come on! Batter up!"

Louie stepped up to the plate. Now that he was batting, the pitcher looked awfully close. But Louie stood there, waggling his bat.

Tony was pitching now. He let fly with a hard one first. Louie was so excited he closed his eyes and swung blindly.

"Strike one!" shouted Harold, as he caught the ball. "No wonder you can't hit it. You've got your foot in the bucket, Fat."

He was right. Louie had stepped back away from the plate as he swung. "Come on, Louie, step into the ball," called Willie. "Don't pull away from it."

Louie set his feet firmly at the plate. He was sure he wouldn't step away again. But every time the ball came at him he pulled away, swung blindly, and missed.

"Strike three!" shouted Harold jubilantly. "You're out. A swing like a rusty gate!" He grabbed the bat from Louie's hands. "Go on, Fat, you're last fielder."

Louie felt awkward, but he trotted off to take his position. He got to bat again, later. Try as he might, he couldn't keep from "stepping in the bucket." He struck out again. But it felt good just to be up there swinging.

When the game broke up, Louie got his precious mitt back. "Bring it again tomorrow," said Willie. "We'll have another game."

"Phew, he's no good," Harold teased. "But we've got to have that mitt. So long, Fat."

"So long, fellows," said Louie.

He ran across the street and pounded up the

stairs. His sturdy legs pumped hard. He pretended he was running for home plate.

Mom was working in the kitchen, getting supper ready. Pop was sitting at the table. Louie hurried to put his mitt away.

"You're back just in time, Louie," said Mom. "Here's a pan of hot water. Now wash your hands and face. I'll soon have a nice big meal ready for you."

Louie noticed that Pop wasn't reading his paper, as he usually did around suppertime. Instead, he was saying to Mom, "So they're going to close the foundry for two or maybe three months. I'll have my job back when they open again. In the meantime I'll have to try some of the other shops."

"And just when you're feeling so well again," said Mom. "Well, Louie will help us now. He started today. He took the laundry down to Mrs. Hertz and brought the money back."

She made Louie feel proud.

Pop said, "Well, well, there's nothing like starting young."

"That's right," said Mom. "Work hard, come home early, bring back the money—that's the way for a man to be."

"A boy has to play hard and exercise, too, Mom. Don't forget that," Pop said.

"I played baseball today," said Louie. "It was good exercise and a lot of fun, too. I wasn't very good at it, but the boys said they'd let me play again. I let them use my catcher's mitt. It's the only one that we have."

Pop nodded his head wisely. "That's the way. Be a good American."

Mom put heaping plates on the table. "Now, Louie," she said, "I want you to eat every bit of that. Whether your pop is working or not, you're going to get plenty to eat, all the time."

Louie sat down and looked at his plate.

"Mom," he asked in a low voice, "do I really have to eat it all?"

"Why, what's the matter with you, Louie? You're not feeling sick?" Mom came around the table and felt his forehead. "Of course not! But I get so worried when I think how we lost your little brothers and your little sister. They were so young when they——"

"Now, Mom, don't carry on so," said Pop gently. "We've got to look after Louie now. He's all we have left. Why don't you want to eat, son?"

Louie felt tongue-tied. He could hardly answer. Then he managed to say, "Because . . . because the kids call me . . . fat."

"Oh, those children!" said Mom. "You mustn't pay any attention to them, Louie. Why, a growing boy has to eat to be big and strong. You'll have to eat and eat until you fill out that frown wrinkle."

As he always did when Mom said this, Louie reached up to his forehead between his eyebrows. He frowned and, sure enough, he felt the wrinkle.

Pop laughed. "That's right, Louie, that's right. You'll have to fill out until it goes away."

Louie grinned, too. He still couldn't forget that the boys called him Fat. But he ate everything on his plate, and a second helping, too.

After dinner Pop stayed in the kitchen, instead of going into the other room.

"Christina," he said, "I'm worried. In this big country there ought to be more people buying pretty iron fences and grilles for their doors and other ironwork. I can make the things, if people would only buy."

"They will, they will," said Mom. "Don't you worry."

"The foreman always trusts me with the hard jobs," said Pop. "But if there's no work for me, what can I do? How can I pay the rent and buy food for you and Louie? How can I buy clothes? I don't know what to do."

"You'll find something to do," said Mom. "We'll get along even if you have to wait for the foundry to open again."

Pop was doubtful. He shook his head. "I don't know what things are coming to," he said.

Louie was listening, round-eyed. "I'll bring home some more money tomorrow," he announced. "Won't I, Mom?"

Mom and Pop had forgotten that Louie was there. They were surprised. Then they both smiled at him.

Mom said, "Certainly, Louie. You may deliver some more laundry tomorrow."

Pop said, "Well, I'll have to do something! I'll give up smoking to save money until I get work again."

Mom looked at the clock. "Come along now,

Louie," she said. "It's half past seven. Time for you to be in bed."

Louie was soon asleep. He dreamed that he was grown-up and had a good job. He came home and handed Mom a roll of bills. Then his dream got mixed up, and he found himself playing baseball.

The next day he could hardly wait for the boys to come home from school. He hurried about the apartment helping Mom. He hauled the laundry in Mrs. Riley's little wagon. Finally the gang began to gather in the vacant lot.

Louie hurried over with his mitt. The boys were crowding around Willie, looking at something he was holding in his hands. They were all pointing and talking excitedly.

"Look," said one boy admiringly. "Ty Cobb!"

"And Frank Chance," said another.

Louie managed to slip into the group to see what was happening. Willie had a lot of little colored pictures in his hands. He was showing them to the boys.

"What are they?" Louie asked Jack, a tall boy beside him.

"Why, they're pictures of big-league baseball players," said Jack. "They come free with penny candies."

Several of the boys reached in their pockets and pulled out some of the pictures.

"I'll trade you an extra Zack Wheat I've got," said one.

"For Ty Cobb?" said Willie. "That's not enough."

Louie had heard of Ty Cobb, a young player, as fast as lightning, and a good hitter. He knew that Frank was a famous first baseman and Zack a great outfielder. Louie began to wish he had some of the pictures, too.

But he seldom had any pennies for candy.

Louie was so interested in the pictures, wondering how he could get some, that he didn't see Harold come up.

Suddenly Harold jumped in front of him and pushed him in the stomach. "Hello, Fat," he said. "Are you going to catch with your stomach again, the way you did yesterday?"

Some of the boys laughed loudly at that.

"What's the matter?" said Harold. "Cat got your tongue?"

Louie was so confused he couldn't answer. He just stood there.

Harold walked up to him again and pinched his arms. "Pretty beefy, I'd say." He pushed him in the stomach again.

Another boy called out, "What's the matter, Fat? You a sissy? You going to let him do that to you?"

"Sure he is," said Harold. He pushed Louie again. This time Louie stumbled backward and nearly fell.

"Fatty is a sissy! Fatty is a sissy!" The chorus grew louder as the other boys took up the cry. "Fatty is a sissy!"

Louie could stand it no longer. He rushed at Harold. In a moment they were rolling on the ground, wrestling furiously. Louie was awkward, but he was strong and chunky. In a minute he had Harold on his back and pinned his arms to the ground. Harold struggled, but could not loosen Louie's hold. The boys crowded around, shouting.

Willie said, "I guess he beat you that time, Harold. Better say 'uncle' to us."

Harold looked around desperately. He struggled again, but Louie held on firmly.

"Uncle," said Harold finally, through clenched teeth. He stopped struggling and lay on the ground, breathing heavily for a while.

When Louie got up, he had an empty feeling in the pit of his stomach. He felt more shaky now than before the fight. Harold got up and brushed himself off.

"Make them shake hands," one boy called out loudly.

"Sure," said Willie. "Go on. Shake hands."

Harold looked angrily at Louie. He was two years older than Louie, though he was no bigger. He didn't like to be beaten. He walked over and put out his hand. Louie took it.

"You're a pretty good fighter, Fa—— I mean, Louie," said Harold.

Louie gulped. "S-so are you," he said. He was feeling better already.

Soon they were playing baseball. Everyone forgot about the fight. After that a lot of the boys still called Louie "Fat," but they weren't so quick to tease him.

Louie Learns a Lesson

It was several weeks before Pop got a new job. It didn't pay much, he said, but he was glad to be bringing home money again. Just as he was well started in his new work, he got sick again and had to stay home a whole month. Louie helped Mom as much as he could. The neighbors were amazed.

"That little Gehrig boy is just six," said Mrs. Riley, "and look how he delivers laundry!"

"Is he that young?" asked Mrs. Cantino, who lived next to Mrs. Riley. "He looks so big!"

Then Pop was well and working again, and all the Gehrigs felt better. One night Pop reached in his pocket and said to Louie, "Here's something maybe you'll want, since you're so crazy about baseball."

He handed Louie two of the little colored pictures of baseball players.

Louie was excited. "Who is it, Pop? What does it say here?" he asked eagerly.

"It says 'Honus Wagner of Pittsburgh' on both of them," said Pop. "I don't know who Honus Wagner is, do you?"

Louie had heard the boys talk about the great Honus Wagner. He had led the National League in batting seven times.

"May I really have these, Pop? Willie and Tony have lots of pictures. They got them with penny candies. Maybe I could trade one of these for . . . for . . . even for Christy Mathewson."

"Who is he?" asked Pop.

"Willie says he's the best pitcher there is," said Louie. Then a thought struck him. Where did Pop get the pictures? He said, "Pop, do you eat penny candies?"

Pop roared with laughter. "No, son," he said, "I got the pictures out of tobacco packages. Now that I'm working again, maybe I'll have some more for you soon."

That night Louie slept with the pictures held tight in his hand. The next day he had a better idea than trading one of them. All summer long he had been trying to learn to bat. He didn't close his eyes any more when he swung at the ball. But he still couldn't keep from stepping back into the bucket. He didn't connect with the ball very often. Once in a while, when he met it squarely with all the force of his chunky body, it went flying out of the lot.

The next day Louie went over to the lot with his mitt in one hand and his pictures in the other. He walked quietly up to Willie.

"Look," he said, holding out his pictures.

"Honus Wagner!" said Willie. "I'd like to have one of these. Want to trade?"

Louie said, "No, but maybe I'll give you one if . . . if you'll show me how to bat."

"Is that all?" crowed Willie. "Here, let me throw you a couple."

Louie ran for the bat. Willie pitched a few easy ones for him to hit.

"You're trying too hard, Louie," advised Willie. "Just take it easy. Take a nice smooth swing. There's nothing to it."

Goose walked up. "Aw, he's too clumsy," he said. "What do you want to bother with him for?"

"I bet I can learn," said Louie boldly. He knew he wasn't so quick as the other boys. But hadn't Mom always said, "Work hard enough and you can get what you want"? So he kept on trying every day to throw and catch and bat. Besides, it was the most fun he'd ever had.

45

Louie wished the summer would last forever, but September came quickly and it was time for school. This year he would enter the first grade of public school.

Mom said, "I'm afraid you won't have much time to play now, Louie. Remember, you belong in school from now on. After school you'll have to help me. I need you to pick up and deliver the laundry."

"Yes, I know, Mom," Louie said. "I'll help you all I can. You know I will. But if I do that, when will I find time——"

"Now, don't worry, Louie. Maybe you can play before school. Some of the other boys work afternoons, too."

That was the way it worked out. Louie got up at five o'clock every morning and slipped across to the vacant lot. There were usually enough boys for a scrub game, and they played until time for school. After school Louie was busy helping Mom until suppertime. When seven-thirty came he was tired and ready for bed.

One October morning Harold and Tony were talking about the World's Series baseball games, played every year between the champion teams of the American League and the National League. Harold was for the Detroit Tigers. Tony was for the Pittsburgh Pirates. Two games had been played, and each team had won one. Louie rushed up. He was eager to hear the news, since he still couldn't read the newspaper.

"Boy, you just wait until this afternoon," boasted Harold. "The Tigers will clean up on the Pirates. Nobody can stop Ty Cobb!"

"How about Honus Wagner?" Tony answered. "I bet Honus Wagner can win the series for Pittsburgh all by himself! He's the best ball player in either league."

Louie listened, wide-eyed, to these older boys who knew all about the big leagues.

"Is that so?" shouted Harold.

From all sides the boys started boosting their favorites. Their talk rang through the neighborhood. Suddenly Goose said, "Jiggers, fellows, the police."

"Golly," whispered Tony, "it's Fishcakes!"

Walking toward them was a husky, blue-coated policeman, swinging his stick. He was a familiar figure in the neighborhood. But he seldom said anything to the boys. What could he want now?

He walked up to the group, which was now standing silent. "Good morning, boys," he said pleasantly.

For once, Louie was the only one who could manage to speak. "G-good morning, Mr. Fishcakes," he said.

The boys could hardly keep from laughing. Harold and Tony turned their backs and held their mouths. That dumb Louie had called the policeman Fishcakes—to his face!

Louie suddenly realized what a slip he had made. He turned as red as a beet. He wished he could sink through the ground. But he had said it now, and there was nothing he could do. There was nothing he could say.

"Well! Fishcakes, is it?" said the policeman. He looked around the group, now frightened.

Suddenly he burst out laughing. "Ha, ha, ha!" he roared. "That's a good one! It's Fishcakes now! Wait till I tell my wife. Ha, ha, ha!"

The boys gave a great sigh of relief.

"Listen, boys," said Fishcakes, "I came over to warn you proper. I like to see you young ones having a good time and playing ball, but you'll have to be a little more quiet. There are some folks who like to sleep later than this. Don't you go breaking any windows, either."

"Yes, *sir*," said Harold.

"Yes, sir," said the rest of the boys.

"I don't like to see young lads get into trouble. I'm warning you *now,* before we have any real complaints. Get along with you, and don't make so much racket."

He started walking up the street. He turned back for a minute to say, "And in case you didn't know it, the Pirates are going to win!"

"Gee, Louie," said Tony, "how could you be so dumb?"

Although he felt relieved, Louie was still too ashamed to answer.

"Why, Fishcakes is a regular fellow," said Willie. "But I'd never have had the nerve to call him that to his face. Whew!"

"Come on, let's get the game going. It's late," said Harold. They all took their positions for the game.

When Pop came home to supper that night, he had a package wrapped up in newspaper. It was a long, thin package. He laid it on the kitchen table and winked at Louie. "Well, Louie, what did you do today?" he asked.

Louie told him about his experience with the policeman.

Pop and Mom both laughed. Finally Louie thought it was funny, too.

"You see, Louie," said Mom, "it's always better to be honest. Don't say things behind a person's back you wouldn't say to his face."

"Now, maybe you'd like to see what I've got in my package," said Pop.

"Is it something for me?" Louie asked.

"Well, let's see," said Pop. "This afternoon, just as I was getting ready to come home, I had a little piece of tin left over. And I thought how boys always like to have something to play with." He pulled off the wrappers. "So I made you a beanshooter!"

"Now, Heinrich, what will Louie do with that?" said Mom. She didn't seem to like it very much. "He'll probably break a window!"

"Not with this, Christina," said Pop. "He can't hurt anything. This beanshooter won't shoot hard enough or far enough to do any harm. Besides, a boy needs some toys, you know."

"Oh, thanks, Pop," said Louie. "May I try it?"

Mom shook her head, but she went to the cupboard and got out some navy beans. "Here you are, Louie," she said. "When you take it outdoors, you had better use little pebbles. You pick up all these beans and save them. I'll wash them off and then I can bake them."

Louie practiced with his beanshooter while Pop read his paper and Mom got supper ready.

He aimed at the doorknob. After a couple of hard blows, he hit it squarely. The bean went *Plang!* and bounced off into a corner. Louie ran over, picked it up and looked around for something else to shoot at.

Louie looked around and saw Pop's coat hanging on a hook. Louie took aim at one of the big buttons. He blew with all his might. This wasn't quite so easy. After a few tries he began to come close. Then he took very careful aim and let fly. *Plunk!* The bean hit right in the center of the button and fell to the floor.

He tried again and again until he could hit the button almost every time.

"Come on to supper, Louie," his mother called.

Louie put the beanshooter carefully behind him on his chair. Later, when he went to bed, he placed it beside him so he could touch it if he wakened during the night.

Early the next morning, even before the boys

were out for baseball, Louie took his beanshooter and went over to the lot. He gathered a handful of small pebbles and tried out a few. First he tried shooting at home plate. That was too easy. He could hit it every time. He looked around for something else. A sparrow was hopping along the fence, twittering and pecking for bugs. "I wonder if I could hit him," thought Louie.

The little bird was jumping and fluttering and pecking. It was hardly ever still. Louie aimed carefully and shot a pebble toward the sparrow. But the little bird had hopped two or three feet away before the pebble hit. Louie tried again. This time it was even worse. The sparrow flew up into a bush, and the pebble bounced against the fence.

Louie never stopped to think that he might really hurt the bird. It seemed a sort of game, like hitting the button on Pop's coat. He crept closer, worming his way across the ground. He put in a smooth, round little pebble, aimed carefully and gave a tremendous puff. The stone bounced right off the bird's head, and the little sparrow toppled over. With a shout, Louie ran up to the spot and reached for the bird.

Then he stopped, his arm outstretched. The bird lay still. Its feathers had been shimmering in the sun. Now they were hanging limp and dull. Louie gulped. Had he killed it? He had never once thought of such a thing. He had only been playing with his beanshooter.

Suddenly a lump came up in his throat. He felt as though he were going to cry, but he forced back the tears. Then he picked up the bird. He shook it a little and spoke to it in a soft voice. It didn't move at all. Then he knew. It was dead. He had killed it.

He felt sorry and ashamed. He put the bird down gently on the ground. He took his shiny new beanshooter and broke it over his knee. He threw it as far away from him as he could. With the bird in his hand, he went over to the fence and scooped out a little hole. Gently he placed the bird in the hollow and pushed dirt over it. He smoothed the earth down.

Then he ran as fast as he could back to the apartment. Mom was getting breakfast. He fell on his cot and sobbed into his pillow.

"What's the matter, Louie? Aren't you playing baseball this morning?" Mom asked kindly.

Louie told her what had happened. She said, "I think you've learned your lesson. I don't think you'll ever do it again. Now come along, Louie. You should be getting ready for school."

The Boys Get into Mischief

ONE CRISP autumn day Willie joined the crowd at recess. He had exciting news. "What do you know, fellows!" he said. "I've got a real, genuine football."

"You're joking." Harold laughed.

"Just wait till tomorrow morning," Willie said.

Before school Willie brought over the ball. Louie found that he could play football much better than baseball. He was so sturdy and his legs were so strong that the other boys had a hard time tackling him when he ran.

Even Harold was impressed. "For such a little kid," he said, "you're pretty good."

Louie grinned a big grin. "It's fun," he said. "But I'd rather play baseball."

Even when winter set in, the boys always gathered in the vacant lot for some kind of game. It was football as long as the ground was clear. When snow came, it was building forts and throwing snowballs.

Mom decided to give up washing for other people. She got a job that took her away from the apartment all day.

Louie didn't know what he should do. "Mom," he said, "when I carried laundry for you and brought the money home, you liked it, didn't you?"

"Why, certainly, Louie," she said.

"What is to be my job now?" he asked.

"I'll tell you what," said Mom. "Maybe you can clean snow off the walks in the neighborhood. When you get a little older, you can get a newspaper route."

"Oh, that will be fun," said Louie. "Every time it snows, I'll go along the street and offer to shovel off the snow."

"Yes, and you must always clean the snow off well, Louie," said his mother. "Then the people will want you to work for them."

So each afternoon Louie walked about the neighborhood with an old shovel. He cleaned off the walks in front of little stores and houses. He soon got a reputation for good work. Almost every evening that winter he brought home some money.

In February there was a cold snap. It snowed and snowed. The mercury in the thermometer dropped to ten degrees above zero. One afternoon as he was leaving school, Louie forgot to put on his extra sweater when he rushed out. He had his mind on a grocery a few blocks away. He might shovel the snow there and get paid well. He ran for his shovel as fast as he could.

Then he dashed to the store. He got the job! It was a long stretch of sidewalk, and the snow was heavy. Louie shoveled and shoveled. Each time he shoveled, he tossed some snow into the gutter. At last he had the walk clean.

After he had finished, he began to feel cold. He collected his money hurriedly and started home. By the time he got up to the apartment, he was shivering.

Mom tucked him in bed after supper. She said, "Louie, don't forget your sweater tomorrow. You really ought to have a good overcoat. But they cost so much! Now go to sleep. You'll feel better in the morning."

Louie slept so soundly that night he didn't even wake up in time to go out and play. When he did wake up, he felt hot and tired.

Mom came in and felt his forehead. "Oh, oh, my little Louie," she said, "you've got a fever. You stay in bed all day today. I'll leave your lunch right here beside you. Now don't move until I come home tonight."

After Mom and Pop had gone, Louie began to think about school. It seemed very strange not to be getting up and going to class. That was where he belonged. Hadn't Mom always told him, "School is where you belong. The only way you will amount to anything is to go to school. It's your duty."

He thought about it. Then he decided he would just show Mom that he wasn't going to lie home in bed when he should be in school. He'd do his duty.

He got up and put on his clothes. He felt a little dizzy. He slipped into his seat at school just as the bell rang. Once inside the schoolroom, he began to feel drowsy. His head was hot, and he could hardly keep awake. In a few minutes the teacher went back to Louie's desk. She said, "You don't seem well, Louie. You go along down to the office."

A few minutes later, he was sitting by the desk of Mr. Halligan, the principal. Louie told him why he had come.

Mr. Halligan said, "Louie, that's a fine spirit.

You're a very conscientious boy, but it's not good for you to be here today. You might get awfully sick. Then, too, some of the other pupils might catch something from you."

Louie nodded weakly.

"I'll tell you what I'll do," said Mr. Halligan. "You go right on home and stay there till you get well. I'll mark you present for today, and for every day you have to miss. Will that make you feel better?"

Louie looked up gratefully and managed to smile. "Thank you, Mr. Halligan," he said.

The principal walked to the door with him. "Now go right on home to bed," he said.

Louie stayed home all day and all the next. The second morning he didn't ache any longer. He jumped out of bed and got dressed in a hurry.

"Are you sure you feel all right?" asked Mom. She put her hand on his forehead. "You don't seem feverish. All right, Louie, go along to school, but come right home afterward. Don't go shoveling any snow today."

Louie came straight home that day, but the next day he felt so well he cleaned the walks at three places. He earned three dimes.

Whenever the weather was warm enough, the boys took the opportunity to get a baseball game started. As they were playing one day late in March, they noticed a strange blue-coated figure walking along the street. He was swinging his billy club.

"Who's that?" asked Tony.

"Oh, that's old Beanpole," said Harold. "Fishcakes got sick and has to stay home for a while."

It soon turned out that Beanpole wasn't so friendly as Fishcakes had been. The very next morning he came over to the lot and said, "All right, you kids, go on home. This is no time to be playing ball while decent people are in bed. Now go along, all of you."

Reluctantly the boys went home. The next day the same thing happened.

"Somebody ought to teach him a lesson," grumbled Harold. "We've got a right to play here if we want to. Fishcakes never bothered us if we didn't make too much noise."

Louie was troubled. He couldn't see why a baseball game was going to bother anybody. He was itching to play. Then he began to think about what Harold had said. Maybe . . .

The next morning Louie did not take his catcher's mitt out with him. Instead he called to some of the boys to come over to the corner. He whispered to them. They listened. Then they all nodded and smiled. They all talked very fast and patted Louie on the back. They went off in different directions. A little later they met again in the alley back of Louie's apartment building. They were carrying bundles.

"Should we do this?" Willie asked.

"Why, sure," said Harold. "What are you afraid of?"

They worked busily for a while, then agreed to meet the next morning.

At five o'clock on a March morning it was hardly light. But a group of boys were busy on the roof of an apartment building near 170th Street. They carried a figure that looked like a man. It was a dummy made of old clothes, stuffed with newspapers. On top of it was an old hat. They boosted the figure up against a chimney, then lifted it up a foot or so off the roof and tied it there.

"Gee," said Tony, "that looks spooky!"

Louie looked at it. It *did* look spooky. He giggled.

"How'd you ever think of this?" said Harold.

Louie didn't answer, but took a coil of wire out of his pocket. The boys stretched it across the roof and tied it tight to a couple of pipes on either side. It stretched there, a foot above the roof. In the morning light it could scarcely be seen. Louie and the boys stood back and viewed their work with pride.

"Hurry up, while it's still dark," Harold said.

Louie gulped. "All right," he said. "You fellows hide now."

While the others scattered to hiding places behind chimneys, Louie went down to the street. There was the patrolman, walking his beat. Louie hesitated. Then he called out, "Mr. Officer, Mr. Officer, come quickly! It looks as if there's a dead man up here!"

Beanpole hustled over. "What's that?" he said. "What's that?"

"Right up here on the roof," said Louie.

He scurried up the stairs, with Beanpole close on his heels. They reached the roof and Louie pointed. In the gray light it surely looked as though a man were hanging there.

Beanpole rushed forward. He tripped over the tightly stretched wire and fell flat.

With a howl of delight the boys burst from their hiding places. They roared with laughter as Beanpole sprawled full-length on the gravel of the roof.

"It's too early to be playing games, Mr. Policeman," shouted Harold.

The boys rushed down the stairs. They went back to their homes, and soon were off to school.

When Louie got home for supper that night, he noticed that his father was sitting at the table, but he wasn't reading his paper as he usually did.

"Louie," he said sternly, "come here."

Louie's heart sank.

"What's this I hear about the policeman this morning?"

In a moment Louie had told the whole story.

Pop looked at him severely. Louie didn't notice how hard it was for Pop to keep from laughing. Mom hovered in the background, looking worried.

"Louie, you know you must be punished," said Pop.

"I . . . I guess so," said Louie.

"I want you to understand about this, son," Pop went on. "You had no right to play such a trick on a policeman. He is paid by the city to keep law and order. Remember that. In this house we obey the law. We're good citizens."

Louie had never thought about it that way before.

"Maybe you thought the policeman didn't

treat you boys right. You should have come and told me or your mom," said Pop. "You know, you might have hurt that officer. How would you like to fall on a gravel roof?"

Louie began to feel very bad. He hadn't meant to hurt anyone. It didn't seem so funny any more.

"Come with me, son," said Pop. "Mom, you wait here."

Into the kitchen they went. Pop closed the door. He gave Louie a good paddling.

"Now the next time you see that policeman, you must tell him you're sorry," said Pop. "We don't want to get a bad name."

"That's right, Louie," said Mom. "Don't go getting in trouble."

Supper was very quiet that night. When they had finished, Louie looked sad and worried. Pop cleared his throat. "Louie," he said, "tell me about it again."

Louie was surprised. He told his story again. Pop started to smile. Then he burst out laughing. Even Mom joined in.

"You were wrong to do it, son," said Pop. "But it's still a good joke!"

Louie thought that grownups were very hard to understand.

The next day Louie went out to speak to Beanpole, but he wasn't there. Instead, Fishcakes was back on the job. The boys didn't have any more trouble. They did break a window one day, but every boy chipped in a little and paid for it. Louie gave a penny he had been saving for candy—for candy with the picture of a baseball player. That was better than having to stop playing baseball altogether.

"Why don't we get up a team?" said Willie one day. "There's a bunch over on Broadway we could play any day."

So they started choosing positions. Louie,

with his mitt, got the job of catcher, with Willie pitching. All summer they had exciting games with neighborhood teams. Afterward, the boys would all go over to the Harlem River to swim.

When Louie told her about it one day, Mom was horrified.

"Louie! You don't know how to swim! You stay out of that river!" she said.

"I can swim, Mom," he said. "All of us kids can. I learned by watching the other boys last summer. It's lots of fun."

"But what if you'd get a cramp or something?" said Mom. "What would happen to you? You'd better be careful."

"Don't worry," said Louie. "There's a policeman who always watches us. The water isn't very deep, and we have a good time."

Louie kept on swimming in the river with his friends. One afternoon he wasn't home by suppertime. Mom looked worried as she worked in the kitchen, getting supper. Pop looked at his watch every few minutes.

"Heinrich," Mom said finally, "Louie never has been this late before. I just know something has happened to him. I'm sure he went swimming in that river. Maybe he drowned!"

Pop looked at his watch again. Then he said, "He ought to be home by now. I wish you could be here all day so you would know what he's doing. But I'm sure nothing's wrong." Still, he didn't look so sure.

Just then there was a knock on the door. Pop looked over at Mom. He was worried, but he didn't want Mom to know it.

He went to the door and opened it. A policeman stood there. It was Beanpole. "Mr. Gehrig?" he said.

"Yes," said Pop.

"Come along down to the station with me. It's about your boy."

Mom hurried up. "Is he all right? What's the matter?"

Beanpole said, "I can't tell you anything. Just come along with me."

"Now Christina, you wait right here," said Pop. "I'll go and see what's the matter. It'll be all right."

He started out the door. Mom sat down, her head in her hands. Maybe Louie *was* drowned! Mom was frightened.

It was a very long half hour for her before she heard footsteps on the stairs. She threw open the door. There was Louie, safe and sound! Pop was walking along behind.

Mom took Louie in her arms. "Oh, Louie, what happened?"

Pop cleared his throat. "Mom, Louie's been a very bad boy. Tell your mother, Louie."

"I . . . I went in swimming without any clothes on, and Beanpole said it was against the law,"

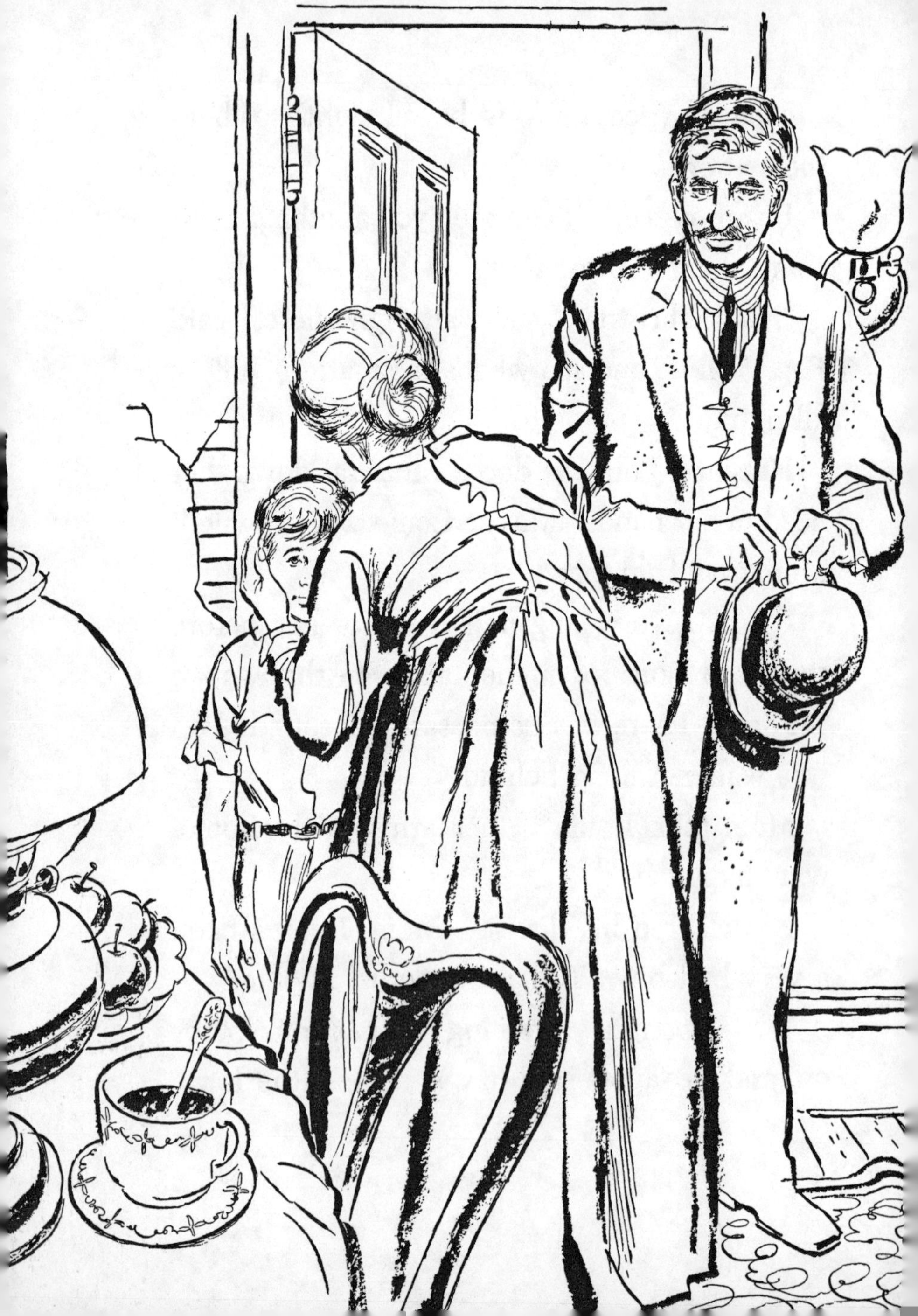

said Louie. "So he took three of us up to the police station."

"Oh, Louie," said Mom, "what happened there?"

"They gave us a good scolding," said Louie. "We didn't mean to do anything wrong."

Pop said severely, "You made the officer angry with that stunt on the roof."

"Pop," said Louie, "I told him I was sorry about that. I never had a chance to do it before today."

"Even so," said Pop, "I'll have to take you into the next room. You know that."

A few minutes later they were back. Pop was still very angry. "In trouble with the police again. At your age! Where will it end?" He fumed and fretted.

Mom said, "Don't be too hard on the boy, Heinrich. Try to remember some of the things you did when you were a boy."

Pop said, "Louie, you've got to be careful. Your mom and I were frightened to death."

Mom said, "Oh, Louie, if anything had happened to you!"

She put her arms around him. Louie still smarted from his licking, but he hugged his mother tightly. It was good to be back in his own home with Mom and Pop. He *would* be careful after this!

Louie Makes the Team

ONE SPRING DAY Willie met Louie at recess. "Harold and Tony and I are going to try out for the school baseball team," he announced.

"Sure," said Harold, "we're nearly in the seventh grade now. They ought to let us play."

Louie thought: "I'm only nine, going on ten. I'm only finishing the fourth grade. I guess I'm too young."

He said, "When does practice start?"

"Next Monday," Willie answered.

When Monday came Louie went out to the schoolyard to watch. Most of the boys throwing the ball around were seventh- and eighth-graders. They were much bigger and older than he. He felt shy. But he noticed that Public School 132 had some old uniforms and a few bats, balls and gloves. He forgot his shyness and gave his name as one of the tryouts. Then he began to practice with the boys.

For two days they practiced, mostly throwing and catching, with a little batting. Then the team was picked. And only Louie of all his gang was selected.

Harold said enviously, "How in the world did you get on, Louie?"

But Louie didn't stop to wonder about that. He was interested only in the team now. He rushed off to the field.

"Louie," said the teacher in charge, "you're the best catcher we've got. You're pretty slow and you've got a lot to learn. But I like the way you keep plugging. Just keep that up, son, and you'll get better."

Louie did hustle. Every place he went, now, he ran. He was sturdy and his muscles were hard from all his work and play and good food and sleep. But he was slow. He must learn to move faster. So he ran on his paper route. He ran to school. He ran on the playground.

When the team practiced, he never wanted to sit down. When he wasn't batting, he wanted to be right behind the plate catching every minute. He tried to learn everything he could. It was a new experience to have a mask and chest protector. Now he could move up right behind the batter without fear of being hurt by foul balls. But there wasn't any left-handed catcher's mitt for him. He still caught with his old mitt because he was used to it.

He soon found that there was a lot more to baseball than he had thought!

He was amazed to find how much there was to learn about catching. He had to give signals to the pitcher, telling him how best to throw to fool the batter. He had to be ready to throw down to second base if there was a player on first trying to steal. Louie's head was spinning with all he was trying to learn, but he soon got better at catching and throwing.

When it came to batting, Louie was discouraged. He just couldn't cure himself of his old habit of stepping in the bucket.

One April day a practice game was scheduled. Louie was surprised and alarmed to see that there were going to be spectators. Willie and Harold and Tony and Goose he didn't mind so much. There were a lot he didn't know, though —children from the other school. Worst of all, there were girls! Goose's sister was there. When she waved to him, his face turned crimson. He felt very shy and ill at ease whenever any of the girls joined the gang walking home from school. And now to have them watching the game!

When it started, Louie had other things to hold his attention. He just couldn't seem to hold onto the ball. The pitcher was in good form. He was sending the ball over the plate with more than his usual speed. Louie gritted his teeth and went after each one as best he knew how. Nevertheless, several balls got past him, and one run was scored when he missed a high outside pitch. When it came his turn to bat, Louie found the opposing pitcher much better than those he had been accustomed to. He struck out three times. Public School 132 lost the game.

Afterward the teacher patted Louie on the back. "You'll do better one of these days, Louie," he said. "I like the way you keep trying. I guess you just haven't had enough experience yet."

The next day at practice Louie found himself shifted to the outfield. Behind the plate, working out with the pitcher, was the regular first baseman. Louie was heartbroken. To lose his place after only one game! But he loved to play so much that he tried just as hard at chasing flies. He practiced swinging a bat time after time, even when there was no one to pitch to him.

"Come on over here, Louie!" called the teacher.

"Yes, sir," said Louie. He ran to the plate.

"Now, Louie," the teacher said, "I want you to keep on practicing catching. I'll put you in every game I can, but we'll have to let someone else start the games until you can get more experience."

So Louie caught for batting practice the rest of the afternoon. He was happy again. He told Mom about it, but she didn't seem to understand. Neither did Pop. But Pop had news of his own to tell.

Fun for Mom and Louie

"Christina," said Pop, "the shop is closing down again. And I've got a good offer to go to Detroit."

"To Detroit?" asked Mom in surprise. "You mean we have to move 'way out there? Why, we can't leave. New York is our home!"

"No," said Pop, "it's only for a few months. I'll have to go alone. But the pay is good and I'll be able to send more money home than usual."

So Mom and Louie were alone most of the summer. One evening while Louie was helping dry the supper dishes, Mom said, "How would you like to go after some eels tonight?"

"That would be great, Mom," said Louie. He

finished the last dish and ran to the cupboard. Standing in the corner was the gig Pop had made. It was a long metal rod with prongs on the end.

"I can stay up late, can't I?" he asked.

"Why, of course," his mother answered. "We can't get any eels until after dark. Did you get the lantern?"

Louie was rummaging in the cupboard. He pulled out a coal-oil lantern and shook it. "It's full of oil!"

Mom looked on her kitchen shelves. "There's only one jar of pickled eels left," she said. "Louie, I can't understand why you don't like them. You like to catch them."

"It's fun to go after them," said Louie, "but when it comes to eating them—th-they don't look so good to me. Do you think we can sell some over at the market? I'd rather do that."

"I think we can," Mom replied as they started down the stairs.

It took them quite a while to reach City Island. It was dark by the time they picked their way to the water's edge. And around them, up and down the shore, they could see lanterns and hear the sounds of other fishermen.

"Here's our place, Mom," said Louie. "And nobody else is here."

He was getting excited. They reached a little inlet where a clear stream flowed through reeds and muddy shallows. It had a firm bank for them to stand on.

"You hold the light, Louie, and I'll have a try," said Mom. "This has always been a good place for eels. I hope we're lucky tonight."

She grasped the gig firmly at the end. She held it high, with the prongs pointed toward the water. Louie held the lantern over the water. He moved it slowly around until he spied a twisting, snakelike body wiggling sluggishly along in the mud. It halted for a moment as the

glow of the light blinded it. Mom saw it, too. She brought the gig down swiftly, and caught the eel just behind the head. It gave a couple of hard wiggles, but Mom lifted it quickly out of the water and flopped it on the bank.

"There's a good fat one," she said, very much pleased.

Louie put the fat black eel in Mom's basket. Then he pulled out the gig and quickly closed the cover of the basket. The eel flopped and flopped.

Again and again they went back to the bank. It wasn't long before the basket began to fill. "Now it's your turn, Louie," said Mom. "You get a couple and it'll be time to go home."

Louie flexed his arm a couple of times. He walked carefully to the bank, holding the gig ready. There was the slightest motion in the dark water, and he stabbed hard. He had one! He pulled it to the bank and beamed delightedly at his mother.

"That's the best one yet, Louie," she said.

Back they went. In his eagerness Louie struck

too soon this time. He almost toppled into the water. Mom quickly grabbed him by the belt and pulled him back. Soon Louie had caught several eels. He rushed back eagerly for more.

"Time to go home, son," said Mom. "We have all we can carry."

"Just one more?" begged Louie timidly.

"Next time you may catch them all," Mom said, laughing. "Now we've got to go home."

They stopped to sell some of their catch. Louie jingled the coins in his pocket and carried the gig. Mom held her basket, which had a goodly supply of eels left. She planned to pickle them and put them up in great jars.

As they were walking along in high spirits, Louie was struck by a sudden thought. "Mom," he asked slowly, "eels and fish are meant to be eaten, aren't they? It's all right to catch them?"

"Why, of course, son. The good Lord put them in the water for people to eat."

"Then they're not like songbirds, are they, Mom?"

"No, son, it's not the same thing at all," she said.

Louie was satisfied. He was also tired when they got home. Staying up so late was very unusual for him. By the time supper was over he was almost always ready for bed. "My boy will never have time for mischief," Mrs. Gehrig used to say, and it was true. Louie always had too many other things to do.

One hot day near the end of the summer Pop returned from Detroit. Now he was called back to the shop to work every evening. There was a big rush order for ornamental grilles. To get them finished everyone at the foundry had to work overtime. Saturday evening Pop said, "Well, Mom, here's some extra money this week. I wish it would keep up all the time."

"I know just what we're going to do with it,"

said Mom. "We're going to Coney Island. Tomorrow!"

"What?" said Pop. "Waste good money on that?"

"Now, Pop," said Mom, "Louie should go there just once, anyway. We don't often have this much extra."

Louie was thrilled at the thought of going to Coney Island. "I would like to go there if we can afford it," he said.

Pop thought it over. Such a holiday was very unusual in the Gehrig household. All three Gehrigs worked as hard as they could. There was usually only enough money for the things that were really needed, like food and shelter.

Finally Pop said, "All right, you and Louie go. I'm too tired. I think I'll sleep all day tomorrow."

So Mom and Louie had a long ride on the cars. The subway train rushed along through a dark tunnel. It carried them under the East River.

They could see nothing out of the windows. Then light began to show in the tunnel, and Louie could see they were going uphill toward the surface. Up and up they went. They didn't stop when they reached the street. The cars went on up an incline to the elevated tracks. This was even better! For many blocks the sprawling apartment houses of Brooklyn were spread out before them.

Coney Island didn't seem like an island at all. It was a huge amusement park built right on the beach at the tip of Long Island. Louie was amazed at all the people he saw. Big and crowded as New York was, Louie had never before seen so many people in one place at the same time. People in bathing suits were packed along the beach. Some ran in and out of the water. Some just lay on the sand. Some were eating and drinking. Some were playing ball. All were having a good time.

Other people crowded around the amusements. There were side shows—the fat lady, the bearded lady, the midgets. There were the booths for ringtoss, rifle shooting, ball throwing. There were rides—the roller coaster, the Ferris wheel, the merry-go-round. There were stands where people could buy things to eat.

Louie and Mom spent all afternoon walking up and down. They tried to see everything.

Louie rode on the merry-go-round, sitting astride a black horse. He smiled and waved to Mom.

Afterward, as they walked along, Louie heard a man shout: "Try your luck! Throw a baseball! Three for a nickel! Step right up and win a Kewpie doll!"

They stopped before the booth in front of which the man was shouting. Men and women, boys and girls were crowding up to the counter, laughing and yelling to one another. At the back of the booth were several shelves lined with little stuffed figures. They were trimmed with wide fringes and painted to look like cats.

"Knock off three, and win the grand prize!" cried the barker, as the man was called. He waved toward an enormous Kewpie doll set up on the counter. It was a fat-cheeked baby doll, with wings and a topknot of hair.

As Louie and Mom watched, several people tried to hit the cats on the shelves. They threw with all their might. But the balls generally sailed right through the wide fringes without touching the figures.

"I bet I could hit them, Mom," said Louie. "I would give you the Kewpie doll."

Mom stared at the funny-looking Kewpie doll everyone was trying to win. What in the world would she do with it? Why would anyone want such a thing?

The barker had heard Louie. He stepped up. "Let the boy try, madam. It's all in fun! Here you are, three for a nickel."

Mom hesitated. All eyes were turned toward her and Louie.

"Let me try, Mom," said Louie.

Mom handed over a nickel. Louie reached eagerly for the three lopsided baseballs. A man next to Louie called, "Come on, son, show us what you can do!" There were approving shouts from the other onlookers.

Louie took aim, but he couldn't forget that the crowd was watching him. He threw the first ball.

Whoosh! It skimmed right between two figures without touching them.

Some people laughed, but there were also cries of encouragement. Louie forgot about the crowd. He just fixed his eyes on the funny little painted face on one of the cats. He threw again.

Plop! The ball struck the figure a glancing blow. It teetered slowly, then fell to the ground.

"Hurrah!" shouted the man next to Louie. He clapped him on the back.

Louie thought, "I can do better than that."

He aimed once more. He pretended he was back on the school field. Now he was throwing down to the first baseman. He kept his eyes glued to the little figure in the middle of the shelf. He threw.

Bang! The ball hit the doll squarely and swept it off the shelf.

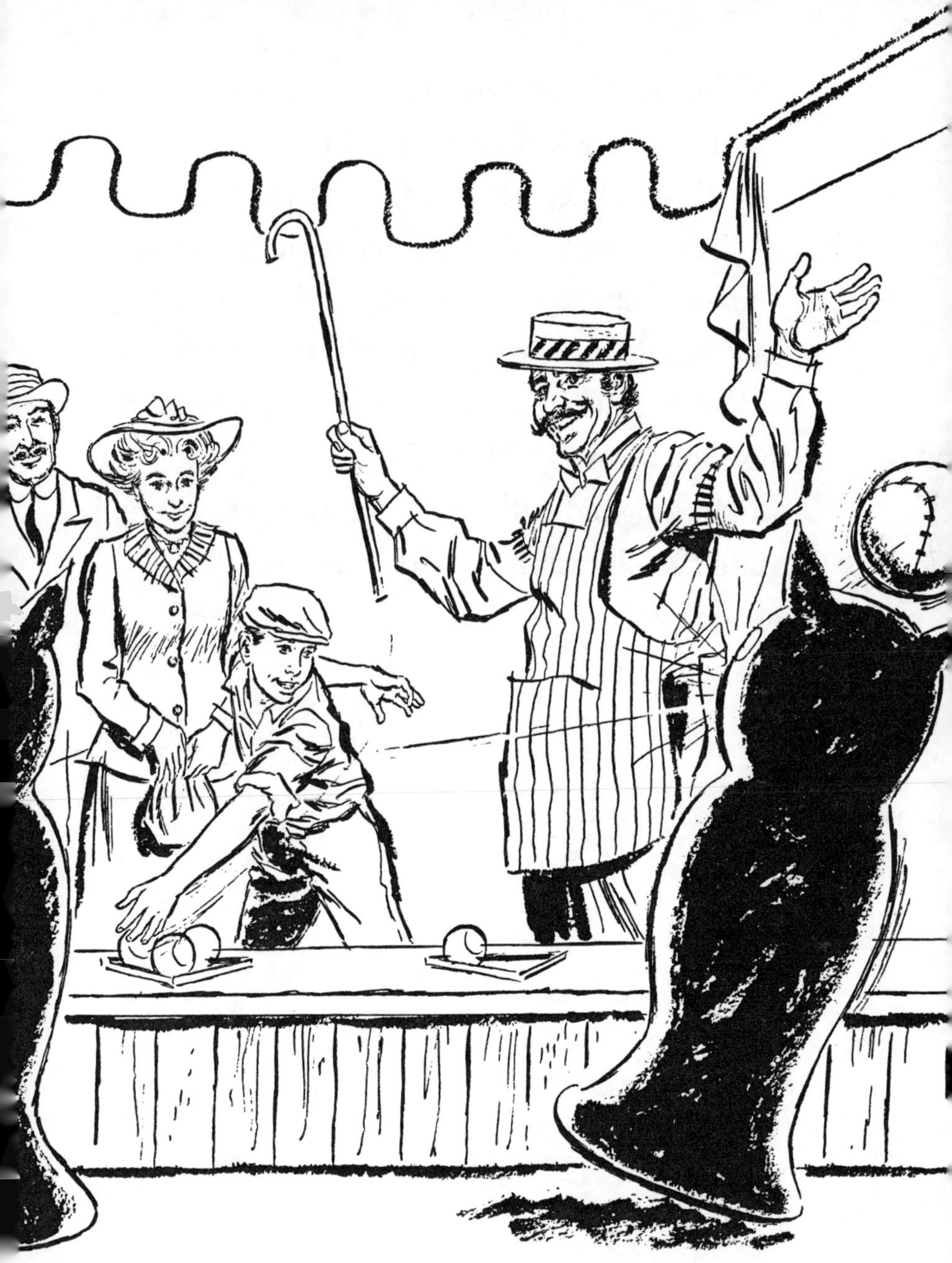

The crowd cheered loudly. Louie grinned at Mom. She looked very surprised.

"Why, Louie," she said, "that was good!"

"Try some more! Just three for a nickel! Give the lad a chance," called the barker. But Mom and Louie squeezed through the crowd and walked on. One nickel was enough to spend, just for throwing baseballs.

Mom sighed with relief. "You know, Louie, I didn't really want that doll anyway!"

Lou Goes to High School

"Good-by, Mom! Good-by, Pop," called Louie, early one morning in May. Mom was on her way across the river to New Jersey where she now had a job cooking. Pop was off to the shop. Louie stretched. He yawned as he set out the food for his breakfast. A bottle of milk. Bread for toast. Jam. Eggs. Louie hesitated between five eggs—his usual number—and six. He felt hungry this morning. Finally he took the sixth.

As he ate, he thought about a plan he had been turning over in his mind. He hated to see Mom leave home so early every morning, travel all the way to New Jersey and barely get home in time to cook supper. If only he could make more money! Well, in a few weeks he would be through with grade school. Then maybe he could get a regular job!

After breakfast, Louie went to the sugar bowl and took out his lunch money—seven pennies. Then he was off to deliver his papers before school. He also stopped at a little delicatessen shop in the neighborhood.

That evening as Mom was cleaning up the dishes, she said, "Well, Louie, just think, in the fall you'll be ready for high school."

"Mom," said Louie, "maybe you won't like this, but I've been thinking. I don't need to go to high school after all."

"What's that?" asked Mom.

Pop pricked up his ears. "Not go to high school!" he said.

"You see, I went into the delicatessen shop this morning. I can get a regular job there as soon as school is over—running errands, sweeping out and learning all about a delicatessen store."

"So!" said Mom. "Maybe you think I'm getting too old to work? Maybe you think I should just stay home and sit in the rocker all day? Pop, did you ever hear such talk?" She acted very stern and looked reprovingly at Louie. Then she laughed.

"Oh, Louie, Louie, you're a good boy, but you can't do such a thing!" she said.

"Why not, Mom?" said Louie. "I . . . I could help lots more that way."

"Now, Louie," said Pop, "don't you get plenty to eat? Haven't we always had a good place to live? Not very big, maybe, nothing fancy, but comfortable?"

"Maybe this winter I could get you an overcoat, Louie," Mom added. "I know you should have had one long ago, but——"

This made Louie suffer. It wasn't what he'd meant at all. An overcoat, indeed! Why, he never got cold. "Mom, you don't understand!" he cried. "There's nothing wrong. I just wanted to help!"

"All right, Louie," Mom said kindly. "We understand. But you must remember this—you are going to high school. Why, in this country everyone can go to school, whether he's rich or poor. It wasn't like that in the Old Country. It's a grand chance that a boy has here. How will you get anywhere when you grow up if you don't go to school as long as you can?"

"Maybe I could have an all-day job just for the summer, anyway," said Louie.

"What! And not get out and exercise? How about your baseball you're so crazy about?" Now Pop was indignant.

Louie hadn't thought much about that. It *would* be terrible not to play baseball. . . .

"No, sir," Pop went on. "A growing boy has to have plenty of exercise, eat plenty, and build himself up. Why, I still exercise at the Turnverein Gymnasium whenever I can. No, sir, if you're not healthy, you can't be a success."

"No, Louie," said Mom. "You go on just like last summer. You can work mornings and play afternoons. But when you go to high school—no more games!"

With only a part-time job that summer, Louie had plenty of time for baseball. He joined a team in the baseball league organized by the Public Parks. He was playing with boys of his own age, and he didn't have any trouble making the team. The summer seemed to go very fast. Before he knew it, August had come and it was almost time to return to school.

When the last league game was over and he was leaving the park, Louie fell in step with Willie, who had been looking on.

"You did fine today, Louie," said Willie. "That last catch was really good."

Louie's face broke into a broad smile. "Thanks," he said. "I just had to get it."

Willie was puzzled. "I can't figure it out," he said. "Do you really have any fun playing baseball? You look as though you're working so hard."

"Why, of course I have fun," said Louie. "How could baseball be anything but fun? I'd like to play a lot better—you know, like a big leaguer."

"You're joking," said Willie, laughing. "Louie Gehrig, 'champeen' batter of the American League!"

Louie blushed. It must have sounded as though he were bragging. "No, I didn't mean I could ever play in the big leagues, but I'd like to be a good player."

"Well, you're much better at football," said Willie. "You've really got the build for that."

"Sure, I like football, too," said Louie. "I like all sports, but baseball is best."

"Going to try for the football team in high school?" asked Willie.

All at once it struck Louie. High school would start soon, and Mom had said there wouldn't be time for games. He began to feel sick at heart. Maybe if he hadn't said anything about the job. . . . Still, Mom knew best. But to give up sports . . .

"N-no, I guess not," he said to Willie. "I'm not good enough, and besides, I won't have time."

"Oh, sure you will," said Willie. "You can't work all the time. They'll be after you, a fellow as big as you are."

A few days later Louie got on the streetcar and went to the High School of Commerce on 65th Street to sign up. At last it came his turn to register.

"What course are you going to take?" he was asked.

"What course?" Louie said. He looked at the teacher with a puzzled frown. "Wh-why, I don't know! I never thought about it before."

"Well, what would you like to learn? What would you like to be?"

Louie sat and thought. Suddenly he smiled. A picture popped into his mind. It had been there for a long time. Where it came from he didn't know. He could see himself in a broad-brimmed hat and heavy boots. He was standing on a hillside by a broad river. He was holding a sheaf of blueprints in his hand. He was talking to a group of men, saying, "Now, men, there's where we'll put the dam."

A voice brought him back to the present. "Let's look over your record. Let's see what your best subjects are? You're a good average student in every class. What studies do you like best?"

Louie spoke up. "I . . . I think I'd like to be an engineer," he announced.

"That will take a lot of hard work, but we can give you the courses to get you started."

So Louie was registered as a freshman. Soon high school didn't seem so big or so frightening. He discovered there wasn't anything so mysterious about the new subjects he was taking. But they were different from anything he had studied before, and it took time to get acquainted with so many new ideas. For the first few weeks he spent his afternoons studying.

One day later on Louie walked over to the field where boys were trying out for the soccer team. They shouted and ran, kicking the ball up and down. Louie stood at one end of the field, watching. He was just itching to try out for the team himself.

Suddenly one of the boys made a wild kick and the ball rolled over near Louie.

"Hi! Send it back!" the boys called.

Louie stepped up and gave the ball a good firm kick. It sailed the length of the field, far out of the reach of the players. One of the boys stood and watched it in wonder. Then he ran over to Louie.

"Say, you ought to be on the team," he said. He was a boy named Oliver who was in some of Louie's classes.

Louie really felt very eager, but he said, "Oh, I wouldn't be good enough."

"When you can kick like that?" asked Oliver. "Come on and try."

"I really can't play well," said Louie. "Besides, Mom doesn't want me to."

"Well, you'd better think it over," said Oliver. "See you later." He ran back on the field.

The next day when Louie was hurrying along to class, he heard his name called. "Hey, Gehrig!" said a tall, good-looking boy.

Louie stopped, and the boy came up to him. "You're Louie Gehrig, aren't you?"

"Yes, I am," Louie answered, nodding his head. He wondered what the boy wanted.

"Come on out for the soccer team. I hear you're pretty good. We need somebody as big as you are."

"Why, I could never make the team," Louie objected. "I like sports, all right, but I'm no good at soccer."

Several other boys crowded around. "Sure you are," said a newcomer. "I've heard about you."

Louie saw that Willie had joined the group. Then Oliver came up, too. In a flash, Louie understood why the other boys were asking him to come out for the soccer team. Oliver had told them what Louie had said yesterday.

"Thanks, fellows, but I know I wouldn't make a good player," said Louie. "Besides, I don't have time. I have all I can do with working and studying."

The boys were getting a little angry. "Well, we can't stand here all day coaxing you," Oliver said. "That's a fine school spirit! My gosh, it can't hurt you to try!"

Louie was troubled. School spirit? He'd like to try, but—— "No, I can't," he said. "Mom won't let me."

"Well, ask her again, sissy," said one of the boys roughly.

"Oh, come on, let him alone," said another.

"Some school spirit!" chimed in a third as the group drifted off.

Louie just smiled and said nothing, but he was feeling pretty bad.

Willie joined him when the other boys had gone. "Don't let them talk like that about you, Louie," he said. "Why don't you ask your mother and father if you can play?"

"No use," said Louie. "They want me to study hard."

He didn't say a word to his parents. Pop was in poor health again and had had to give up his trade. Mom and Pop now worked together at one of the fraternity houses at Columbia University, on Morningside Heights.

When he first heard about it, Louie wanted to know right away what a fraternity house was.

"Well," said Mom, "it's like a boardinghouse, only it's a kind of club. There are many of them around the university."

"You can work there in your spare time, too, Louie," said Pop. "You can wait table and help Mom in the kitchen."

"My, those boys need looking after!" said Mom. "So many of them so far away from home!

"Someday you'll go to college, too, Louie," she went on. "You'll have to, if you're going to be an engineer. This is certainly a wonderful country!"

Louie thought about the soccer team, but he didn't say a word.

"So study hard, Louie. Get busy on those lessons right now."

Back at school, things weren't any easier. Every day one of the boys who had asked him to try out for soccer would ask him if he'd changed his mind. More of the boys found out about it. Louie had to listen to much criticism for his lack of school spirit. Some boys laughed and sneered at him. But Louie was determined. He just smiled and went on his way, though he didn't feel like smiling at all.

"Can't you really play, Louie?" asked Oliver. "Why don't you speak up for yourself?"

Louie explained again.

"I'll bet you could find time to get your lessons done and still play," said Oliver. "You don't want to get a bad reputation around here. Come on, let's talk to the teacher about it."

Louie would rather have slipped out of the room, but as he and Oliver were leaving they met the teacher at the door. Oliver told him about Louie's problem.

The teacher said, "Louis, sports have a real place in school life. It's true that a boy who is a good athlete ought to try out for the teams. If you can't play, you can't, and you shouldn't be criticized, of course. But why don't you talk to your parents again, and see if you can't work something out?"

Louie agreed. On the way to the fraternity house he figured out that he could get most of his lessons while he was riding on the streetcar. He could do the rest in odd minutes when he wasn't helping Mom and Pop. He told them his plan and what the teacher and the boys had said.

"Oh, no, Louie, you ought to spend all your spare time studying," cried Mom. "Remember, you're in high school now and you want to be an engineer."

Back in Germany where Mom and Pop had grown up, only the richer boys could enjoy sports. Dueling with swords was the most popular sport in the universities. There were some hiking clubs and gymnasium classes, but their only object was to develop strength. The idea of teamwork and school competition was hard for Mom and Pop to understand. They did not know what Louie meant when he talked about learning to be a "good winner" and a "good loser." "School spirit" was a new term to them.

Still, Pop was anxious to have Louie do things the American way.

"Now, Mom, maybe the boy's right," said Pop. "Louie played ball at Public School 132, and he passed all right. And if these games are so important in school, he ought to be in them."

"That's right, Mom," said Louie eagerly. "Don't you think I could try it for a while to see how I get along?"

Mom stopped and thought a minute. She wanted Louie to work hard and be successful.

"I don't know, Louie," she said slowly. "You're a big boy now, and it seems like such a waste of good time."

Louie gulped.

Pop said, "You know how these college boys like to play on the teams, Christina—or watch them if they can't play. And our Louie can play."

Mom was impressed. She had her heart set on Louie's going to college. She wanted him to be just like the American college men. And the boys round the fraternity house were always talking about some team or other, some sport or other. Maybe Pop and Louie were right. . . .

"All right, Louie," she agreed suddenly. "You try it!"

Louie was very happy. "And I'll help you and Pop just as much, too," he assured her. "You wait and see!"

He turned up for soccer practice the very next day. Some of the players were still annoyed with him. Some of them called him "Mamma's boy." Louie only smiled. He really felt like smiling now! When the boys saw how he could play, they soon quit teasing him.

Louie did not think much of his own ability. He was really surprised when the coach made him halfback on the team.

Though he had been good at soccer, Louie felt doubtful about himself when the baseball season came around. He was itching to be out on the diamond again, but something held him back. Maybe they wouldn't let him play. Maybe he wasn't good enough. After all, he was poorer at baseball than at any other sport. He wondered if anyone would accuse him of lack of school spirit if he didn't show up for the first day of practice. He didn't know what to do! So he let the first day go by.

The next day, in the hall, he saw a man striding toward him. He recognized Coach Duschatko.

"Gehrig," he said, "I want you at baseball practice today." He said it kindly, but very firmly.

It was all Louie needed. "Yes, sir," he said. "I'll be there."

That afternoon Louie went out to the field. The school lot was crowded with boys tossing balls back and forth. Louie stood by himself over at the side. Finally Coach Duschatko noticed him.

"Haven't you got a glove, Gehrig? Here, take this one and limber up."

The coach walked away, and Louie gratefully joined in with several other boys throwing the ball around. Soon the coach got several "pepper" games going—one batter knocking out short grounders or flies to four or five fielders. He strolled around the lot watching the groups in turn. He was picking out the best players.

Every boy was hustling hard after every ball, eager to be chosen for the team. Louie jumped for the high ones. He dug for grounders. When it came his turn to bat, he concentrated as never before. "Keep your eye on the ball. Meet it squarely," he kept telling himself.

For a week the whole group continued to practice in the schoolyard. Then on Monday morning there was a list on the bulletin board of those chosen to make up the squad. The rest would have to try next year. Louie looked down the list anxiously. Then he saw his name: Gehrig, L. He was on the team! Now, if he could only win a regular position!

The coach was ready when the boys assembled that afternoon. "You'll get your uniforms this afternoon," he said, "and we'll go over to Central Park to practice. This lot isn't big enough. Other days, we'll use a field up in the Bronx. All right, let's start."

All the way over to the park Louie worried about that long ride up to the Bronx for practice. Still, that would give him more time for studying. And surely he could get back in time for supper.

When they reached the diamond, the coach quickly set the pitchers and catchers to warming up. He sent one group to the outfield. A batter was to toss up the ball and knock out flies to them. Louie went along with them. Every time a ball came in his direction, he went after it with all his might. Once the batter sent a long one far over his head. Louie turned and sprinted back, back. He turned just as he saw the ball coming, leaped high in the air and grabbed it. As he came down, he got his legs tangled up. He tumbled to the ground, but he held onto the ball.

He got up and trotted back. "Good catch!" said the boy next to him. "You certainly go after them. Say, my name's Al McLaughlin."

Before Louie could reply, he heard his name called. "Gehrig!" It was Coach Duschatko. Waving to Al, Louie loped in to the infield and reported to the coach.

"Gehrig," he said, looking at his list. "Let's see, what's your first name? Louis. All right, Lou, we need another infielder. You're a good big boy, and a left-hander, too. I want you to try first base. How about it?"

"Yes, *sir!*" said Lou with enthusiasm. He put on the mitt the coach gave him. A real left-handed first baseman's mitt! At last!

He trotted to his position. The coach knocked out grounders to the infielders in turn, and they threw to first. It was up to Lou to run to the base, catch the ball and start it "around the horn"—relaying the ball around the bases. Pep it up, snap it up, keep the ball moving—that was the way to play infield.

When it came Lou's turn to field a grounder, he had to make the stop, throw to second as if for a double play, and then race to first to get the return throw. The first time he picked up the grounder all right, but he didn't get back to first in time to catch the return throw. It went flying off into space.

"Speed it up, Lou," was the coach's only comment.

After a few more grounders the coach called a halt. "It's a little unnatural for you, Lou, isn't it?" he asked.

Lou said that it was. He felt awkward standing out there trying to guess what to do next, and trying to do it quickly.

"The first thing you've got to do, Lou, is to get to that base in a hurry, if the ball isn't batted to you," the coach said. "And when you're there, get ready to step out with either foot, in the direction closest to the throw. When you see where the throw is coming, step out and stretch as hard as you can. But be sure to keep your back foot on the bag. The better you grow at that, the more runners you're going to catch on close plays. Practice it by yourself, until it becomes second nature to you."

Lou understood well enough. Doing it was another story. He got his feet tangled up. Sometimes he stepped too quickly toward the throw, only to have it go to the other side before he could change his position. He blundered and charged around the bag, until some of the players gave a few amused chuckles. But he kept on trying. He was determined to master this new position.

The coach kept watching Lou very closely. He noticed all the blunders and mistakes that Lou made. He noticed that the other players sometimes laughed at Lou. But most of all he noticed that Lou kept trying very hard.

Soon the coach called out, "That's enough, boys. Let's have some batting."

The boys all came to wait their turns to practice batting. One player at a time tried to hit the ball far out in the field. Some players, at the coach's suggestion, tried to bunt the ball, to make it drop gently in front of the plate.

Waiting his turn, Lou practiced running to an imaginary first base, turning and getting set for the throw. Over and over he ran back and forth, back and forth.

"Take it easy, Lou," said Al, who also was waiting his turn at bat.

Lou gave him a big grin. "I'm afraid I've got a lot to learn about first base."

"The way you're going at it, you'll have it all down before the day is over!" said Al.

Of course Lou didn't. But he improved

slowly, very slowly. As fast as he learned one thing, there was another he had to practice. He stuck to it with a will and, when the 1917 season opened, Lou, the youngest boy on the team, was playing first base with Commerce High. But as excited as he was about the team, something else happened that spring that almost made Lou Gehrig forget baseball.

Trouble in School

ON EVERY side Lou had begun to hear talk about the Germans, who were at war in Europe with England and France. He heard about ships being sunk and innocent people killed. Then the boys began whispering to one another when he came around. He could tell they weren't saying pleasant things about him. He couldn't understand it. Maybe Pop would know what was wrong.

One night he heard Mom say, "There are terrible things going on in the Old Country."

"That's what's bad in Germany," Pop answered. "All the time those Prussians want to fight. The people just follow them. I'm glad we're over here now."

"What if the United States fights Germany?" said Mom. "My, that would be terrible! But *we're* all good Americans now."

"Why, Louie, if we were in Germany, they'd have you in the army right now, a youngster like you," said Pop. "There'd be no more school and no more sports."

Lou said, "Some of the boys at school are calling me names like 'Dirty German' and 'Filthy Hun' and 'Murderer' and——"

"They can't do that!" protested Mom. "You're as good an American as anyone. Born right here in New York. You tell them so!"

Pop nodded, but he was worried.

Soon a day came in April when President Wilson asked Congress to declare war against the German government. Everyone in the United States was excited. Everyone was telling stories about the cruel German soldiers in Belgium. Many people started blaming Americans who had German names. They were so excited they had to blame someone near by, though the real troublemakers were far away.

For several days at school it got worse and worse for Lou. Only a few boys really called him names. But many more kept away from him and showed they didn't trust him. The same thing happened to the other boys with German names.

One afternoon Lou walked out on the school lot after his last class. He saw a group shouting and talking loudly about the war. "I wish I could enlist," said a big boy named Eddie. "I'd show that Kaiser and all those Germans!"

"There are plenty of them around here," cried a little fellow who was nicknamed Shorty. "Why don't they go back where they belong?"

"Here comes one now!" shouted Eddie.

"Where do you think you're going, you dirty Hun?"

Lou felt stiff with anger, but he didn't say anything. He started across the yard toward the gate.

"Come on, fellows! Let's get that German!" called Shorty.

The crowd rushed toward Lou. He turned to meet them. For a moment it looked as though they were all going to jump on him. But something in Lou's quiet, determined manner stopped them.

"What are you afraid of?" called Eddie to his followers. "He's a German all right, and probably a dirty spy!"

Lou spoke up stoutly. "That's silly. You know I'm not a spy. I'm as good an American as anyone. I was born right here in New York."

"Yah, up in Yorkville with all the other Heinies," Shorty jeered back.

"Come on, let's jump him," said Eddie. But the boys eyed Lou's size and strength, and no one moved.

"What's the matter? You afraid to fight?" another boy said to Lou.

"No, I'm not afraid to fight," said Lou. "I just don't want to fight you fellows. But you have no right to call me those names."

"So you *are* afraid," shouted Eddie, suddenly becoming bolder. He punched at Lou. As if at a signal all the other boys piled on him, hitting and pushing. There were so many of them that Lou was forced back. He struck out at them, but they kept on coming. He fell back more and more until he could go no farther.

Lou was pinned up against the fence. He struggled to free his arms. He hit out hard at the milling group attacking him. His weight and muscle drove the boys back, but not before he had taken a good pummeling.

"What's going on here?" came a sudden voice. It was the coach.

The group stood around rather sheepishly. Finally Eddie spoke up. "Aw, we're teaching this German a lesson. We're fighting Germany now, and he's probably a spy."

The others nodded.

"You're not exactly using American tactics," said the coach. "Look at the bunch of you jumping one boy. Is that fair play? You fellows are just excited. If you stopped to think for one minute, you'd know better."

"I don't care, he's a German!" insisted Shorty.

"I'm surprised at you," said the coach. "He's a good American and you know it. Every family in the United States came from some other country at some time because they wanted freedom and equal rights. That means you and you and you." He pointed at each one. "When you act the way you're acting, you're tearing down

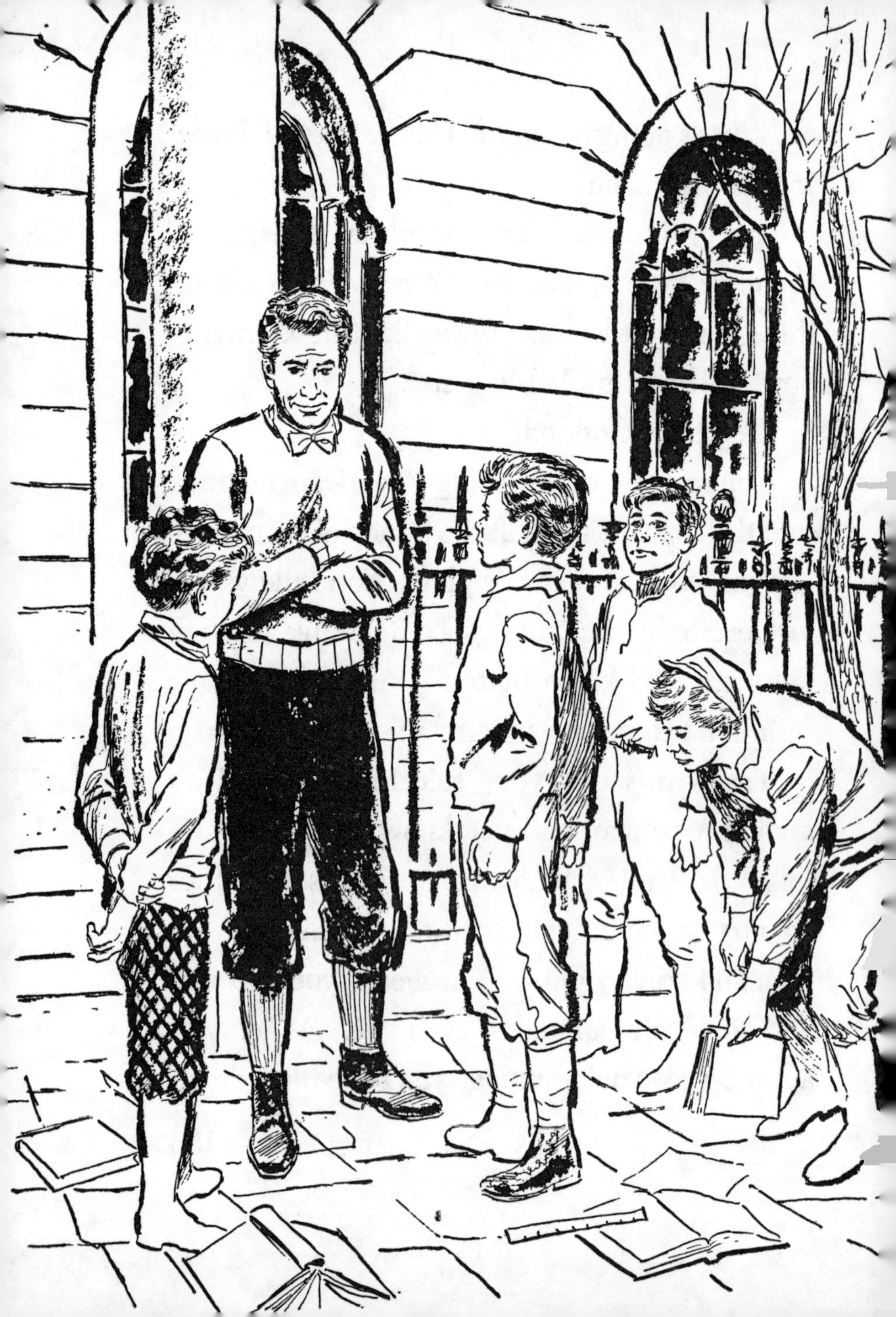

the most important beliefs we have. Think it over, boys. Let's not have any more of this."

Lou was grateful to the coach, but he went home feeling sad and lonely. He couldn't understand why people had to act that way. Why did being German make him different?

Before the war was over, he had more than one bad time with hotheaded boys. More than once he had to fight. But gradually his unfailing good nature brought about a better feeling. The German scare died down. People realized that the enemy was across the ocean, and that there were better ways to fight a war than brawling and calling names.

Lou was thankful to turn his attention back to school, work and sports. Especially sports. He never felt so good as when he was playing on a team. It was easy to forget his troubles in the excitement of playing hard, doing his part with the other boys to win a game.

The coach was relieved, too. "I'm glad this foolish German stuff has stopped," he said to one of the teachers. "Lou's got his smile back."

Out on the diamond Lou thumped his glove and shouted, "Come on, fellows! Let's get 'em out!"

Lou Earns Five Dollars

It was the following spring, and the team had assembled for the first practice of the season. All the fellows were talking as they waited for practice to start. "How do you like the new coach?" asked Al McLaughlin.

"He's fine," said Bunny Bunora, the shortstop. "He really knows baseball."

Lou nodded. "Let's get warmed up," he said. He started throwing the ball back and forth with Al and Bunny. It felt good to be on the field again with a glove on his hand.

"All right, fellows, infield practice," called Harry Kane, the new coach. Al put on his catcher's mitt, and Lou and Bunny took their places on the diamond.

Coach Kane knocked out grounders to the infielders. He was sizing up the team. He wanted to learn how each boy played. Many a time that year he shook his head over Lou. The big boy would lumber in to field a bunt and swing around slowly to toss the ball to the pitcher. But there was something about the way he loved the game and the way he tried . . .

"Lou," said the coach a few days later, after batting practice, "you could really be a powerful hitter. I'll tell you what we'll do. I'll pitch to you fifteen minutes every day and see where we get."

Day after day the coach worked with Lou. He showed Lou how to stand. He patiently tried to cure Lou's old fault of stepping in the bucket. He taught him how to hit curve balls. He told him how to guess what kind of ball the pitcher was going to throw. No matter how much Kane tried to show him, Lou was always eager for more.

One day Commerce had a game at the field in the Bronx. It dragged on and on, as both teams fought hard to win. In the last of the eighth inning, Commerce got three runs to put them ahead, 6-3. But in the top half of the ninth, the other team started hitting, too. Before they were out the score was tied at 6-6.

After the last runner went out at first on a close play, Lou slammed the ball down into the ground. Then he hurried over to the bench and flung down his glove in a rage. He picked up three bats and swung them wildly. He muttered to himself.

Coach Kane came over, surprised. "Lou," he said, "this is the first time I've ever seen you lose your temper. That's not going to help us win the ball game."

Lou selected a bat and pounded it on the ground.

"We can beat those fellows, Coach," he said. "But do you know what time it is now?"

"What time it is?" asked the coach, puzzled.

"If this game lasts much longer, I'll be late for work," Lou said angrily. "Mom and Pop won't have anyone to help them."

"H'm," said the coach. "Let's see you go out there and break this tie, then."

The Commerce pitcher, first up to bat, struck out. Then Bunny went to bat. The opposing pitcher worked hard on him, for he was a good hitter. Finally the count stood three balls and two strikes. Lou fidgeted at all the time this took. The next pitch was called a ball, and Bunny was on base with a walk. Al hit a deep grounder to the first baseman. He was thrown out on a close play to the pitcher, who covered the bag, but Bunny went down to second.

Lou stepped up to bat, still fuming. On the first ball pitched he took a heavy swing and missed. Then he realized he would have to forget about being angry and think of nothing but hitting the ball.

The next two pitches were balls. Then came a slow curve. Lou hit too soon and drove a foul far down the right-field line. He watched the pitcher carefully. It looked as though he were going to throw a fast ball. Lou got set. Sure enough, the pitcher let one go hard and fast right over the plate. Lou swung and met the ball squarely. It went flying on a line right over second base for a safe hit. Bunny was off with the crack of the bat and had crossed the plate with the winning run before the center fielder could throw the ball home.

Lou was all smiles as he trotted back to the bench after running out his hit.

Coach Kane slapped him on the back. "That's

the way to meet the ball, Lou," he said. "We'll have to be late every game if it will make you hit like that."

Lou rushed for his streetcar. Once safely on it, he pulled out his books and set to work on his lessons for the next day. He reached the fraternity house just in time for his evening chores.

That summer, as usual, Lou looked around for a baseball team he could join when he wasn't working.

"Why don't you go up to the Minqua Club?" Al McLaughlin suggested.

"What's that?" asked Lou.

"It's just a neighborhood club organized by one of the political parties," said Al. "But they're going to have a baseball team. Uniforms and everything."

"That sounds pretty good," Lou said. "Is there a regular league?"

"I don't think so," Al answered. "They play

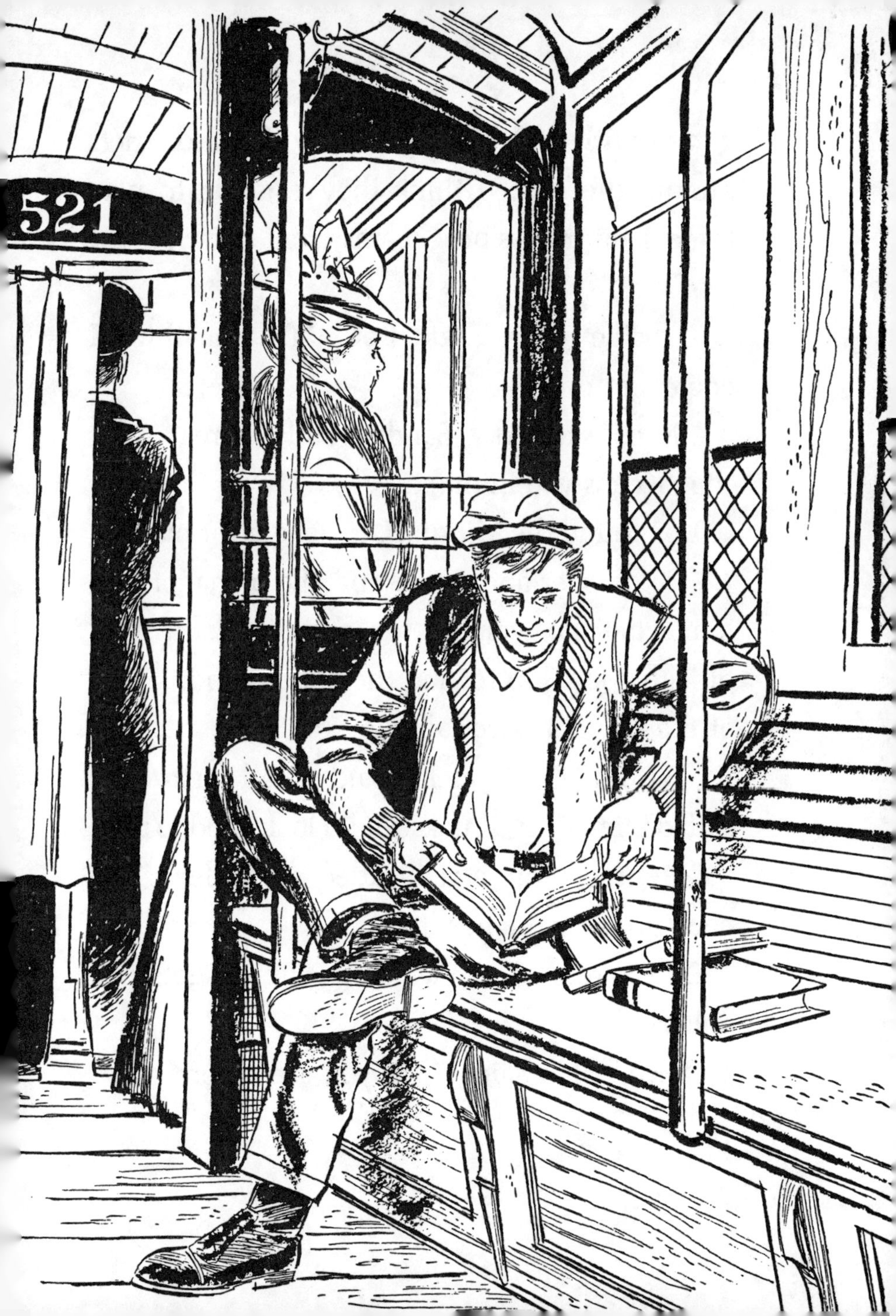
521

games with clubs from other political districts around the city. I think they're going to play some semiprofessional teams from New Jersey, too."

"I'd like to try," said Lou. "Do you think I could get on?"

"Sure," said Al. "Sandlot ball is great stuff, too. Keeps you in practice."

Lou found the Minqua Club eager for players.

"Go on over and warm up," the manager told him when he went to the practice field. Lou quickly joined in tossing the ball around. Some of the players were talking.

"Wish I could pitch," said a tall lanky boy called Slim. "Five bucks would look good to me."

"Me, too," said a redheaded outfielder. "We need another pitcher, too."

Lou asked, "You mean the pitcher gets five dollars?"

"Sure," Slim said. "Are you a pitcher?"

"Why . . . why . . . sure," said Lou, quickly making up his mind. He had become better at throwing than at anything else in baseball. After tryout, the manager gave Lou a chance to pitch several games for Minqua. Lou was given a five-dollar bill after the first game. He rushed home to show it to Mom and Pop.

He was the happiest boy in the world. His parents didn't expect this money, and he would surprise them. Lou dearly loved his home and his mom and pop who worked so hard for him. Someday he'd give them everything they wanted. Now the five dollars looked like a mighty big present for them, and, just think, he'd got it from the thing he loved best, playing baseball!

Mom couldn't believe her eyes. "You mean you got *money* just for throwing a ball?" she asked.

"Well," said Pop, "maybe this baseball is all

right, after all. Didn't I tell you, Mom, that he ought to play?"

But Mom still could not understand. "Is it really honest to get money from baseball?" she asked.

"No," said Lou, "I expect old Beanpole will be after me any minute." But he couldn't keep a straight face. His grin gave him away.

"Louie, Louie, don't make fun of your mom," she protested.

"I'm going to pitch every game I can, and I'll get five dollars every time," said Lou. "Why, the professional ball players make big salaries. Thousands of people go to see them play."

"I can't understand that," said Mom, "but I can understand the five dollars!"

City Champions

"WE'RE GOING TO have a real team this year," said Charlie one day. Charlie was the sports reporter for the school paper.

It was Lou's last spring at Commerce. A number of students were watching the baseball team practicing for its first game.

"You bet," said Willie. "We might even win the city championship."

"Who do you think is our best player?" a freshman asked.

Charlie looked wise. "I say Bunny Bunora. As a shortstop, he's a wonder. He's a good dependable hitter, too."

"How about Lou Gehrig?" Willie wanted to know.

"Well, he can do more things than any other player on the team," said the reporter. "He plays first base, or outfield, or pitches—wherever he's needed."

"Is he big!" exclaimed the freshman.

Willie said, "Lou's grown at least three inches this summer. He must weigh two hundred now, and I'm sure he's six feet tall."

Charlie scribbled some notes. "It's funny," he said. "He's not a natural baseball player. Too awkward. But when it comes to football . . ."

"He still likes baseball better than anything," said Willie. "He plays in sandlot games every summer, I know."

"Maybe that's why he's improved more than any player on the team," Charlie said. "Besides, the coach has been working hard with him."

"He's the most ambitious fellow I ever saw," said Willie. "When he isn't playing some game or going to school, he's working. He practically earns his way. He helps his family a lot."

"Sounds like a Mamma's boy to me," said Charlie, "but he *is* a good athlete."

"Doesn't he ever go out at night?" asked the freshman.

"You've got him all wrong," said Willie. "He's no sissy. He's just shy, even though he's so big. He gets his fun playing games. And he's willing to work for the chance."

"Look at that!" shouted the freshman. Lou had hit the ball into right center field.

"When he connects, he really gives the ball a ride," said Willie.

"They'd better watch out for Commerce this year!" said Charlie.

"Yes, we'll show them all how to play baseball this year," Willie said.

As the season went on, the other teams did have to watch out for Commerce. Lou and his teammates won most of their games. Commerce was fighting hard for the high school championship of Greater New York.

In the final game which would decide the championship, Commerce played its main rival, Commercial High School of Brooklyn. It was a close game, and Commerce won it, 6-5. Lou made one error, but he made up for it with two timely hits, one a double.

After the game Bunny and Al and Lou and the other boys were laughing and slapping one another on the back, when Coach Kane signaled for silence.

"Boys," he said, "I have an important announcement to make. I know you're all happy over winning the championship, and you should be. You played a good game and deserved to win. But——"

Here he held up his hand again, for Lou, in his high spirits, was jostling Bunny, and Bunny was jostling Lou.

"But," went on the coach, "the season is not over!"

He paused to be sure they'd listen. What could he mean? The boys looked at one another. The season not over, when they had won the championship?

Coach Kane laughed. "I won't keep you in suspense any longer," he said. "As champion of the high schools of New York, we've been invited to play the champion of the Chicago high schools—in Chicago, on June twenty-eighth!"

There was dead silence for a moment. Then shouts of "Hurrah!" and "Bring them on!" and "Let's go, fellows!" rang out. Then there was one question after another.

"When do we leave?"

"Are we going on the *train*?"

"How long will we be gone?"

"What team will we play?"

Finally the coach signaled for quiet again. "I can see that no one is afraid of any team in Chicago. But remember, it will be a tough game. They play good baseball in the Chicago schools."

Again there were shouts of "We'll beat them!" "New York can beat Chicago any day!"

Then Al, who was captain of the team, spoke up. He asked a question that was worrying several of the boys, especially Lou: "Do you think our parents will let us go?"

"I'm sure they will," said the coach. "Tomorrow I'm going to give each of you a sheet of paper with all the information on it: when our train leaves, how long we'll be gone, everything. I'll want you to take it to your parents and get their permission."

"Which school in Chicago won the championship?" asked Bunny.

"It hasn't been decided yet," said the coach. "So far as I know, three schools still have teams in the running."

Excitement ran high as the boys discussed their coming trip. To go to Chicago! Hardly any of them had been very far away from New York before. To play the Chicago champions! Why, it would be almost like playing in the World's Series!

But Lou was still worried. How could he be away that long? What would happen to his work? Who would help Mom and Pop? But he *must* go, somehow. He didn't say anything that night to Mom and Pop. When he had his sheet with all the information, he told them about it.

"What's this? What's this?" said Mom. "You want to go all the way to Chicago? To play baseball? I've never heard such a thing!"

Lou's heart sank. "But, Mom," he said, "I'm sure I could get someone to help you while I'm gone. And . . . and, gee whiz, I wouldn't want to miss this for anything in the world!"

"It isn't the work, Louie," said Mom. She could never get used to calling him Lou. "But to be away from home for five days! Who would look after you? Who would see you got your meals? Who would see you went to bed? Why, you've never been away from home!"

Lou was stumped. Imagine worrying over things like that! "Oh, Mom," he said, "I'm not a baby!"

Pop had to laugh. "You're pretty big for a baby, son." But even he was disturbed over such a long trip. "I think you'd better listen to your mom, Louie," he went on. "You can play baseball right here in New York without going way out to Chicago."

"But you don't understand!" Lou argued. "This is a championship game! The Chicago champions against the New York champions!

And Coach Kane is going with us and several other teachers besides. And, gee, we'll get along fine!"

But Mom was a little frightened by it all. "No, Louie," she said, "my mind is made up. I'd never rest for one minute worrying about you. Anything else you want to do, I want you to do But this is too much."

Lou was in the dumps. Not to go to Chicago with the team! Not to play in the big game! But Mom was firm. "It's for the best, Louie," she said. "You tell Mr. Kane to let some other boy go."

When he told the coach the next day, Lou was heartsick. But he didn't complain. He just said his parents thought he ought not to go.

Coach Kane looked at Lou. He looked at his long, sad face. "Cheer up, fellow!" he said. "I'm going to have a talk with your parents myself. Let me see what I can do."

Lou was so worried when he and Coach Kane reached the apartment that he could hardly speak. He was relieved when the coach suggested that Lou wait for him while he spoke to Mom and Pop alone. Lou took him in and called Mom out of the kitchen. Then he went outside and fidgeted.

Time seemed to stand still. Maybe Mom was right. Maybe he really shouldn't go. After all, it was just one game. But he'd rather go than do anything else in the world. Why, he'd be all right. Why should Mom worry about him like that anyway? With Coach Kane and so many others going along, nothing could happen.

Just then the door opened. Coach Kane looked out. He was smiling broadly. "Come on in, Lou," he said.

Lou's heart skipped a beat. "You mean . . ." he faltered.

"Yes, Lou, you may go," said Mom. "But——"

Lou didn't wait for any more. He rushed over and kissed her.

"Well, I'll be going," said Coach Kane. "Thank you, Mr. and Mrs. Gehrig. Don't worry about a thing!"

"Such a nice man," said Mom after he had gone. "He promised to see that you were tucked in bed every night and——"

"Oh, gosh, Mom," protested Lou, "did you tell him to do that?"

But he didn't worry about it for long. He was going to Chicago!

The Big Game

AN EXCITED, happy bunch of boys boarded the train at Grand Central Station the next Wednesday. At last they were on their way to Chicago for the big game.

The shouts of their fellow students were still ringing in their ears. Hundreds of pupils had all ridden down to the station in big buses. The band had played right up to the minute when the gates at the station clanged shut. After the boys had looked through the train from first car to last, they ate a big dinner in the dining car. Then they began to talk about the game.

"I wonder how good this Lane Tech team is,"

said Al. "They must be pretty good to win the Chicago championship."

"We won the New York championship," said Rossomondo, the second baseman. "New York is bigger than Chicago, so we ought to be better."

"Do you think there will be a big crowd at the game?" asked Lou.

"Listen to Lou," Rossomondo laughed. "He's worrying about the crowd already. Why, sure, there'll be a big crowd."

The others began to tease Lou. Finally Lou grinned. When the coach returned to the car, the boys were having a gay, noisy time.

"All right, boys," said Coach Kane, "that's enough. Time to quiet down."

The boys scattered to their berths. "Come on, Lou," the coach said. "I've promised to see that you get to bed safely."

For once Lou was too happy to feel bashful.

"I'm surprised at you, cutting such monkey-shines," said Mr. Kane. But he was smiling, and there was a twinkle in his eye.

Chicago was strange, but all the boys insisted it wasn't so big or so interesting as New York. The game was set for Saturday. On Friday they got a chance to practice. It was good to be out on the ball field again. They were soon feeling more at home.

They practiced with a will. They peppered the ball around and got used to the diamond and the way balls bounced in the infield. They limbered up at the plate. They clamored for more batting practice when the coach stopped them.

"No, that's enough for today," he said. "Save your hitting for tomorrow. Besides, the Lane boys have to use the field now."

As they were going to the dressing room, they saw the Lane Tech players come onto the field and start their workout.

"Gee," said Al, "they look pretty good."

"I hear they've got a red-hot pitcher," said Bunny.

"Oh, never mind," said Rossomondo. "So have we." He punched their pitcher, Jacobs, playfully. "Don't you know Jacobs is good enough to pitch for the Yankees?"

"Whew, look at that hit!" said Lou. A Lane player had lined the ball against the wall.

Back in the dressing room Coach Kane said, "I want to tell you boys something today, and then let's forget about it. You're playing a good team. But they're just nine boys like yourselves. You've played good teams before. When we go onto the field tomorrow, I don't want you to be thinking about how good they are. Just play your game the best you know how, and you'll do all right. I have confidence in you. I'll be satisfied with you, win or lose. But remember—we came out here to win!"

In spite of the coach's warning, the boys were nervous the next day when they warmed up. A big crowd was filing into the stands. Never before had the boys played with so many people watching them.

"All right, boys, that's enough," called Coach Kane. He led them back to the dressing room. He talked to each one.

"Arm feel all right, Jacobs?" he asked the pitcher. Jacobs nodded.

"Don't work too hard the first few innings,"

the coach continued. "Just pace yourself the way I've told you. McLaughlin," he said to the catcher, "slow him down if he gets to pitching too fast."

"Sure, Coach," came back the answer.

"Now, Strom," said the coach, "you've got a pretty big field to cover in this park, but don't play too deep. And Troy and Starke, be careful on any balls that bounce against the wall. Remember, they'll bounce back hard off those bricks, so allow yourselves plenty of room.

"Gehrig," he said, "we may get a lot of sacrifice bunts today, so be on your toes. You'll have to move in fast, but be sure you have that ball before you try to throw it."

Lou nodded.

Soon instructions were over, and the boys were trotting back on the field. At the same time the Lane boys appeared on their side. A great cheer went up from the spectators.

For a moment shyness almost got the better of Lou. All these people! Maybe he should have stayed at home! How could he go out there before this crowd?

Suddenly Coach Kane was walking along beside him. "Lou, how about asking your mother to give me some of those eels she was pickling?"

"Do you really mean it, Coach?" asked Lou, feeling better at once.

"Sure," said the coach. "Don't forget me when we get back home. All right, fellows, let's play ball. Bunora, you're up first!"

The game was on!

It was a tight struggle. First Commerce took the lead, then Lane tied it up. Neither side was playing its very best, for both were a little nervous. But there were brilliant plays, too. Every boy tried hard to bring victory to his team.

Lou was still bothered by the big crowd, not so much when he was in the field, but when he was batting. He played well at first base. He accepted every chance without an error. But he couldn't make a hit. Four times he went to the plate without getting a good "piece" of the ball. He was fretting and worrying about it. He wasn't doing his part. He was letting the team down, he thought.

His teammates piled up eight runs. Lane Tech fought back hard and managed to score six runs. So the score stood 8-6 in favor of Commerce as the boys from New York came to bat in the first half of the ninth inning.

Coach Kane gathered them about him for a few minutes before the inning started. "Good going, boys," he said. "Now let's go out there and get some more runs. There's just one inning left, and our lead isn't safe. Let's get some more runs for insurance. These Lane fellows are dangerous. With any luck at all they could make two or even three runs this inning."

"We'll get them, Coach," Al McLaughlin, the captain, promised. "Come on now, fellows, let's get out there and play!"

There were five batters ahead of Lou that inning, and he was afraid he wouldn't get another chance. Starke, first up, hit to the second baseman and was thrown out. Lou's heart sank. One out. Then Troy smashed a safe hit to center. Christman, the Lane fielder, let the ball go through his legs. Troy put on a burst of speed and went all the way to third.

The Commerce boys cheered, but Coach Kane suddenly jumped to his feet and ran to the base line. Christman had thrown the ball back to the infield. The Lane second baseman was standing on the base, holding the ball and shouting to the umpire, "He's out! Didn't touch second!"

The umpire agreed. He waved Troy off the diamond. Troy came back to the bench, very downcast. Lou's heart sank again. Two out now.

Then Jacobs went to bat. He got a walk on four straight balls. Bunny came up and hit a hard grounder to the shortstop. All the Lane boy had to do was toss the ball to second, and the inning would be over. But in his eagerness to make the play he fumbled the ball. Jacobs and Bunora were both safe. Johnson, the Commerce third baseman, came to bat and drew a walk. The bases were full! Two men were out in the ninth inning! And it was Lou's turn to bat.

"All right, Lou," said the coach. "Bring them in. You can do it. Just meet the ball squarely."

Lou walked to the plate. He took his stance. He waggled his bat a couple of times, eyed the pitcher. The Lane boys were shouting encouragement to one another. "Here's an easy out!" called the first baseman.

"Hasn't had a hit all day," chimed in the shortstop. He pounded his glove. "Come on, let's finish him off quick!"

"Pour it right in there," the second baseman yelled to the pitcher. "Strike him out!"

Lou straightened his cap, shifted his feet. He *had* to get a hit now. The pitcher wound up and threw. Lou let it go by. "Ball one!" called the umpire.

Lou could hear the big crowd talking excitedly in this tense moment. "Strike him out!" they called. "The bigger they come, the harder they fall!"

"Cut him down to size!"

Big, husky Lou felt very small and very much alone standing at the plate in huge Wrigley Field. But he felt very determined, too. "You can do it," Coach Kane had said.

Lou got set for the next pitch. It looked like a ball, but at the last second it curved sharply over the corner of the plate. "Strike one!" called the umpire.

Lou swung hard at the next pitch and drove

the ball foul on the ground down the first base line. Strike two. He let the next two go by; both were high and outside. Three balls, two strikes. The next pitch would tell the story. The crowd was standing. Lou gripped his bat and watched the pitcher carefully.

The Lane boy wound up and let fly. The ball came straight for the plate, about waist-high. Lou cocked his arm back, then swung into the ball with all his strength. *Crack!* He hit it solidly. It shot out toward right field like a bullet from a gun. The Commerce runners raced for home. The Lane right fielder dashed madly back toward the wall.

Legging it for first as fast as he could go, Lou watched the ball rise higher and higher. He couldn't believe his eyes. It was going over the wall! A grand slam home run! Four runs in!

A great roar burst from six thousand throats. "Yeah, Gehrig!" they were shouting.

"Some wallop!"

"Boy, is he a Babe Ruth!"

Bunny and Jacobs and Johnson were waiting at the plate as Lou trotted in. They shook his hand and clapped him on the back. The crowd kept cheering. Lou grinned broadly. Somehow, he didn't feel shy any more.

"That was a beauty, Lou," said the coach.

"We've got them now, Coach," said Lou happily.

And the game ended 12-6 in favor of Commerce, for, after Lou's crushing home run, the Lane boys were easy outs in their half of the ninth.

Back in New York the students waited to greet the team at Grand Central Station when it arrived. That morning the *New York Daily News* had printed Lou's picture. His face was round and smiling as it was when he crossed the plate after his home run. Under the picture were the

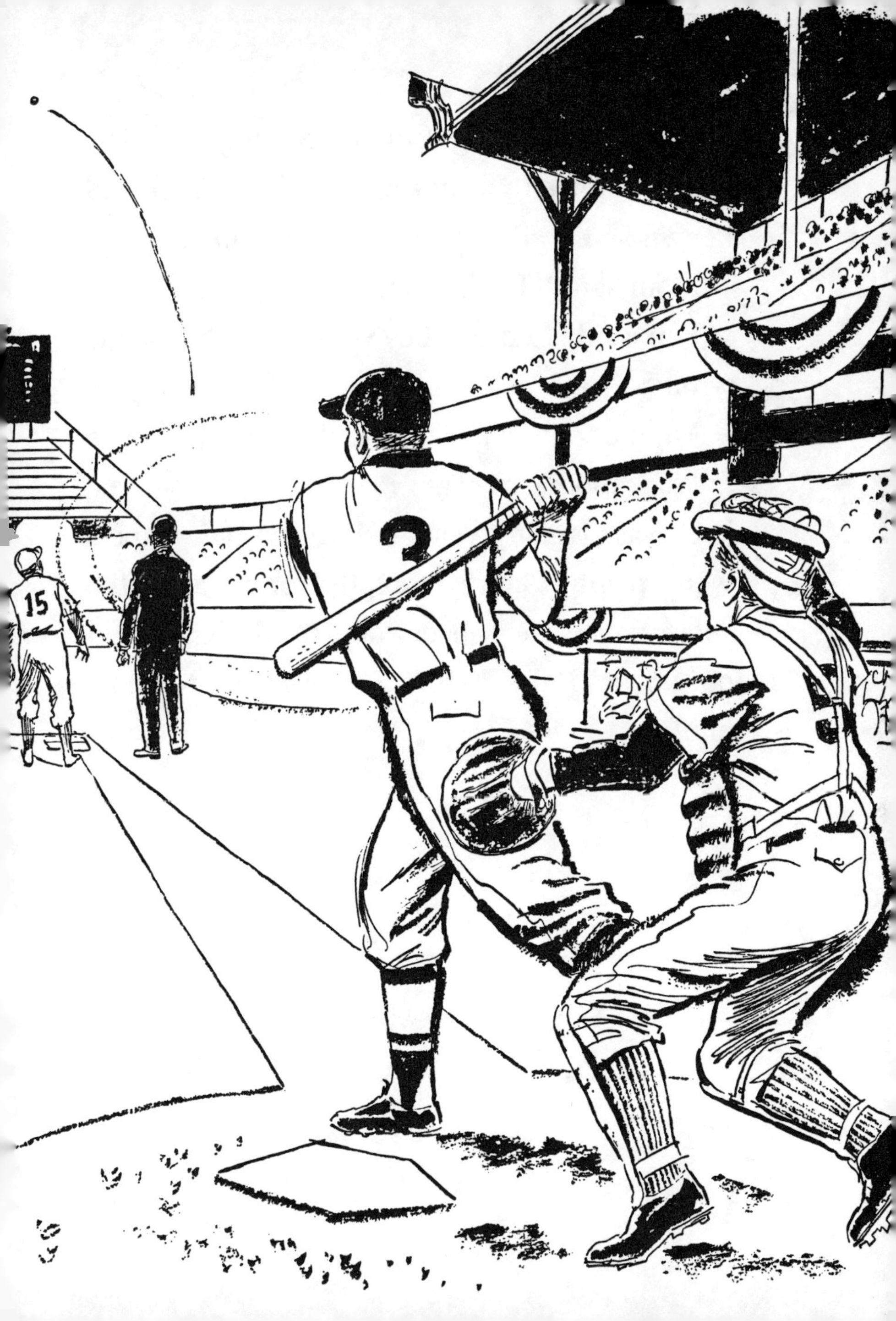
15
3

words "Louis Gherig, Commerce Slugger." The article referred to him as "the New York lad known as the 'Babe Ruth' of the high schools."

Mom said, "Look, Pop. It's our Louie!"

Pop said, "Look, they've spelled his name wrong!"

Mom asked, "Who is this Baby Ruth they're talking about, anyway?"

It wasn't many years before the newspapers were spelling Gehrig correctly, for it was on the sports pages nearly every day. And Mom found out about "Baby Ruth." She even got to know him!

The Yankee Slugger

It was a warm day in Philadelphia the afternoon of June 3, 1932. In Shibe Park, home of the Philadelphia major-league baseball teams, a big crowd was gathering. The New York Yankees were to play the Philadelphia Athletics. The Athletics for three years had been champions of the American League.

The stands were full of fans from New York. They had come to see their beloved Yankees play. But they were outnumbered by the Philadelphia rooters, who were sure Connie Mack's boys would beat the New Yorkers. There was a lot of good-natured argument back and forth.

A man from New York said, "The Yankees are in first place now. It will take more than Philadelphia to stop them!"

A storm of protest arose from the Philadelphia fans near by.

"Where were the Yankees the last three years?"

"The season's young yet. Just you wait!"

"Watch out today! Earnshaw will stop your home-run hitters!"

On the field the game was starting. All eyes were turned toward the diamond. Big George Earnshaw was pitching for Philadelphia as the Yankees took their first turn at bat. The first man up, Saltzgaver, got a base on balls, and the Yankee fans cheered. Then Earl Combs grounded out, and there was a cheer from the Philadephia fans. Then the great Babe Ruth came to bat. Ruth ten times had won the Amercan League championship for hitting home runs. He had tied for the lead two more years. Babe was trying hard, but he swung three times without connecting. He shook his head and walked to the bench. The crowd was noisy.

"Two out now!"

"Earnshaw will stop them."

A tall, strongly built player walked to the plate for New York. He stepped into the batter's box, set his feet carefully. He grinned at the Philadelphia catcher and waggled his bat. It was Lou Gehrig!

"Come on, Lou!" the New York fans shouted. "Hit it over the fence!"

Gehrig swung. He hit a tremendous drive far out toward the flagpole. The Philadelphia fielders just stood there and watched it. The ball sailed over the fence in deep left-center, beyond the flagpole, for a home run.

Lou trotted around the bases. He modestly tipped his cap to the spectators who cheered wildly as he crossed the plate. He was grinning as he went back to the bench. New York led, 2-0.

"We can always depend on Gehrig," said one New York man to another.

His companion nodded. "That's right. Lefty Lou never lets us down. He plays harder than anyone else on the team. And do you know he hasn't missed a single game since he started with the Yankees in 1925?"

"I don't see how he does it," said a rooter.

"He had almost no experience when he came to the Yankees," said the first man. "Why, he had to quit college to earn money to help his family! He wanted to be an engineer, but he had to give it up."

"That's right, and he played only a short time with Hartford. But I've heard the Yankee scouts had their eye on him ever since he hit a home run in a high-school game in Chicago."

"Lou was pretty raw to start with," said another, "but he worked so hard nobody could take his place. Now he's the best first baseman in either league."

The New York fans quieted down then. Philadelphia had scored two runs to tie the score.

In the third inning Gehrig came to bat again. He watched Earnshaw getting ready to throw, he got set and—*smash!* He hit the ball on a line toward the right field wall. Up . . . up . . . and over! Another home run! New York was ahead for the second time. The fans clapped as Gehrig came trotting across home plate.

A Philadelphia rooter rubbed his chin. "That Gehrig is good!" He sighed.

"He surely is," called a New Yorker. "He tied with Babe Ruth last year for the most home runs. Forty-six he hit!"

The Yankees got another run that inning, but Philadelphia came back with six, to lead 8-4. In the fourth inning the Yankees started to hit. Earl Combs hit a home run. Then Babe Ruth hit one high and far over the fence for another home run. Lou Gehrig came to bat.

"I guess he's had enough for one day," said

the talkative New Yorker. "But I wish he'd do it again."

No sooner had he finished speaking than Gehrig connected for a terrific hit. The ball went deep into the stands in left-center. When the shouting quieted down, one of the New Yorkers pulled out his record book.

"Look! Look!" he called. "That's the fourth time Gehrig has hit three home runs in a single game! Nobody *ever* did that before!"

"I met Gehrig once," said another man proudly.

"You did? Is he just as quiet and shy as he seems on the field?"

"Yes, sir! You'd never know he was a great baseball player. He was as pleased as Punch when I said I liked his playing. You'd have thought I was his best friend. But he didn't say much. He just smiled and said 'Thanks.'"

A woman in the party spoke up. "He's given

his mother and father a lovely home—in fact, everything they could want," she said. "They used to be very poor."

"He's a great team player," said her husband. "All the players look up to him. And he doesn't even realize it!"

Gehrig came to bat in the seventh inning again. New York was behind, 10-9. The Philadelphia team had a new pitcher, now, Mahaffey.

Lou was cheered as he walked up to the plate. "Make it four, Lou! Hit 'er over the fence!"

Gehrig took his stance. This was a game the Yankees had to win. He watched the new pitcher carefully. Lou was studying the way the man threw. There was one ball, outside. Then a strike, over the outside corner. Then another ball. The next pitch looked good to Lou. He swung sharply and hit a whistling liner toward right field. The Philadelphia fielder stood helplessly as the ball sailed over the fence.

For a moment the crowd was silent, stunned. Then a mighty roar rose from the stands. They cheered and cheered, long after Gehrig had crossed the plate happily and was thumped on the back by his teammates.

Hoarse and excited, the New York fan waved his record book, pointing to it. "Four home runs in four times at bat!" he managed to shout. "Why, nobody's done that since Bobby Lowe in 1894! Let's see, Ed Delehanty hit four home runs in one game in 1896, but not in succession. And no one else! Oh, you Gehrig!"

"Not even Babe Ruth has hit four in one game," said another.

"What a man!" agreed the Philadelphia rooters. "What a man!"

Down on the field Lou trotted out to his position at first base. He was as earnest and hard-working as ever. He'd never had so much fun in his life. He still marveled at the fact that he was playing first base for the great New York Yankees. He could hardly believe it, even now, when he had just hit four home runs.

"Let's go, fellows!" he called. He thumped his glove and waited for the next play.

The Yankees won the game. They won the flag that year, and the World's Series. They beat the Chicago Cubs four games to none. And Lou? He hit three home runs in the World's Series and batted .529!

"The Greatest Example"

It was the Fourth of July, 1939. The Yankees were playing a double-header with the Washington Senators. In the big stadium far up in the Bronx more than sixty thousand people crowded into the double-decked stands. It was more than a holiday celebration—more than just a good day for baseball—it was Lou Gehrig Day!

The crowds pushed into their seats. They were all talking about Lou's retirement from baseball.

"There'll never be another like the Iron Horse," said a man in a first-row box.

"Just think, he played in two thousand one hundred and thirty consecutive games. Why, nobody will ever come close to that record!" said his friend.

"Look, there's the 1927 team come back for Lou's day!" The first man stood up to see better.

"Yes," said his friend, "that was the first Yankee team to win four straight World's Series games when Lou was a regular."

A band from the Seventh Regiment was parading smartly across the field. Behind the band marched Lou's old teammates of 1927: Babe Ruth, Bob Meusel, Waite Hoyt, Wally Schang, Benny Bengough, Tony Lazzeri, Mark Koenig, Jumping Joe Dugan, Bob Shawkey, Herb Pennock, Deacon Everett Scott, Wally Pipp, George Pipgras.

When they all had reached the flagpole, the players formed a square. While the band played, the championship pennant of 1927 was run up on the flagpole. The crowd cheered loudly. The procession marched back toward home plate.

"Where's Lou?" asked the man in the box.

"Oh, he'll be out in a minute," said his friend. "Say, how many world's champion teams has he played on, anyway?"

"Let's see, it's here in today's paper," said the other. "He played in seven World's Series, and the Yankees won six of them."

"I know he was captain of four straight world's champion teams," said his friend.

"And listen to this." The first man read on: "He played thirteen full seasons for the Yankees, and part of another. His batting average for all those years was .340. He hit four hundred and ninety-four home runs in all. What a man!"

"I don't see how he could go on being so good even when he was injured," said his friend. "He fractured his hands seventeen times, and still went on playing."

"He would have taken himself out of the game if he wasn't playing well, too," said the first man. "In fact, he often did, after a few innings."

"Here he comes!" A great shout went up from the crowd. Everyone jumped to his feet. Around home plate the players from both the Yankees and Senators were lined up with the band and the 1927 players.

From the dugout walked Lou. He was bareheaded, and wore his baseball uniform. His face was serious. There was not a trace of his usual smile. In fact, he was so choked with emotion he could hardly speak. He thought, "What have I done that all these people are cheering so hard for me?"

He wondered why he couldn't smile. He knew he wasn't sad because he was retiring from baseball. He knew he wasn't sad because doctors had advised him it was time to stop playing. But the great cheers from all these people for him—Lou Gehrig—was such a wonderful thing he did not know what to make of it.

Lou walked up to the plate. There were speeches, and more cheers. Then he received a big silver cup from his fellow players.

Mayor Fiorello LaGuardia of New York City spoke last. "You are the greatest example of good sportsmanship and citizenship. Lou, we're proud of you."

The applause was deafening. It was Lou's turn to speak. He was so overcome, he didn't think he could say a word. Babe Ruth moved over and threw an arm around Lou's shoulders. He whispered, "Say, Lou, does your mom still make those good pickled eels?"

Lou had to smile at that. He nodded back yes and stepped up to the microphone. He could talk now.

He thanked them all for their kindness. He told them he had enjoyed playing baseball more than anything else. "What young man wouldn't give anything to mingle with such men for a single day as I have done for all these years?

"You've been reading about how I'm retiring. Maybe you think it is a bad break. But today I think I'm the luckiest man alive."

Up in the press box the sports writers were writing down everything for their newspapers. One said, "I've never seen anything so fine on a baseball field before in my life. And I've been covering games for many years."

His neighbor said, "That's because Lou is always simple and kind, always brave and loyal. No matter how successful he has been, he has never changed. Everyone loves him—and he didn't know it until today."

Lou walked off the field with Mayor LaGuardia. The little mayor had to look up to talk to tall, husky Lou. Lou had to bend over to hear him. The crowd laughed good-naturedly.

"Lou," the mayor was saying, "I hope you've given some thought to that job we talked about."

"Yes," said Lou, "and I'm deeply grateful for your offer. Of course, the season isn't over yet, but——"

"No rush, Lou," said Mayor LaGuardia, "but you'd do a wonderful job. I know you've had many offers that would bring you more money, but you know how much we'd like to have you."

"Mr. Mayor," said Lou, "I'm going to refuse everything else. I want the chance you've offered me to be a member of the parole board of New York City. I'd like to work with unfortunate lads who are trying to get a new start in life. If I can lend a hand to some of the boys who weren't so lucky as I, I want to do it."

Mayor LaGuardia beamed. He shook Lou's

hand. "That's great!" he said. "That's just wonderful. You're a good citizen, Lou."

"I know that many of the kids who grew up on the streets of New York the way I did have had a tough time," said Lou. "Some of them I remember have got into trouble, all because of a bad start. They didn't have a home like mine, a mother and father like mine. I want to do my share to help them."

"Come and see me when the season's over, Lou," said the mayor, as he went to his box. "The sooner you can start, the better."

"I'll be there," said Lou. He walked back to the dugout. The Yankees took the field for the first inning.

"Come on, fellows, we've got a game to win!" shouted Lou from his seat on the bench.